The Getting *Unstuck* Workbook

The Getting *Unstuck* Workbook

Practical Tools for Overcoming Fear and Doubt— and Moving Forward with Your Life

Britt Frank, LSCSW

A TarcherPerigee Book

tarcherperigee

an imprint of Penguin Random House LLC
penguinrandomhouse.com

Most TarcherPerigee books are available at special quantity discounts for bulk purchase for sales promotions, premiums, fund-raising, and educational needs. Special books or book excerpts also can be created to fit specific needs. For details, write: SpecialMarkets@penguinrandomhouse.com.

Paperback ISBN: 9780593713211
eBook ISBN: 9780593713228

Printed in the United States of America
1st Printing

Book design by Laura K. Corless

for M. M. and S. D.

CONTENTS

Author's Note . . . ix

Introduction . . . xi

Part 1: Cracking the Procrastination Code: *How to Break Bad Habits* . . . 1

Part 2: Who Are You? *How to Make Friends with Your Mind* . . . 53

Part 3: Humaning Is Messy: *How to Create Skillful Relationships* . . . 83

Part 4: Decluttering Your Inner Closets: *A Compassionate Approach to Self-Awareness* . . . 137

Part 5: Probable Impossibilities: *Getting the Life You Want* . . . 189

Acknowledgments . . . 223

Suggested Reading . . . 225

No book can fully cover the breadth and depth of human complexity. My worldview is filtered through the lens of privilege as a cisgender white woman living in a Western culture. The information and exercises in this book assume you are currently in a safe enough environment, with access to food, clean water, and basic life necessities. There are no positive affirmations, journal prompts, or "thought work" exercises that can solve problems related to an oppressive environment. This book does not address situations in which abuse or systemic failures are present, nor does it discuss challenges related to sexuality, gender, or social injustice.

There are as many reasons for feeling stuck in certain situations as there are humans, so please take what's useful from these pages and leave the rest. Science is often subject to change without notice, so although efforts were made to ensure the accuracy of all information as of this book's publication date, future scientific research may render current best practices inadequate or inaccurate.

The information in this book is not intended to replace therapy or be a substitute for mental health treatment. Always check with a medical doctor to rule out medical causes before assuming a symptom has emotional or psychological origins. It is important to note that human responses are sometimes mistakenly labeled as pathology when they are a result of neurodivergence. This book includes information about trauma, addiction, abuse, and other topics that may be triggering to some readers. Use your discretion, and if you feel unsafe or uneasy with any of the exercises or topics, immediately stop. You can call or text 988 to reach the Suicide and Crisis Lifeline, and you can visit www.thehotline.org for domestic violence support. If you are currently unsafe, please call 911 or go to your nearest emergency room.

Have you ever seen someone walk into a spiderweb? If you didn't know there was a spiderweb causing the flailing arms and vocal outbursts, it would be easy to assume that something was *seriously* wrong with that person. But they are neither crazy nor suffering from a case of acute onset arachnophobia. They walked into a spiderweb. They're going to flip out. And that makes sense.

You make sense too.

The most common question I've heard from every client I've worked with—regardless of age, gender, or symptom—is, *"Am I crazy?"* The answer to that question is a resounding "No—you are *not* crazy." Your anxiety, overwhelm, burnout, and stress are *reasonable responses* to the unseen spiderwebs of life. Even the most extreme and severe mental health challenges make sense in context. There is no such thing as a "crazy" person.

Why Listen to Me?

As a licensed psychotherapist who has sat with people for more than a decade, I could tell you the story of a financially reckless person who went on to create their dream business. Or the story of a person trapped in a cycle of abusive relationships who finally broke free. There's the person who starved herself, hated her body, and smoked meth (acquired by doing unspeakable things) who later became an amateur circus performer. The list could go on. What do they all have in common? They're not client composites or case studies. Those stories are all parts of *my* story.

I was an emotional disaster for most of my early life, particularly in my twenties. Fueled by a steady diet of coffee, drugs, and cigarettes, I spent many years willfully ignoring the chaos surrounding me 24/7. I wasn't about to admit the truth to myself—let alone go to therapy—but when I stumbled upon *The Artist's Way* by Julia Cameron, something began to shift. *Working through* that book—rather than simply *reading* it—created the momentum I needed to make significant changes. After finding my way out of that mess (with a lot of help and a brief stint in a religious cult), I went back to school and became a licensed psychotherapist—a journey that ultimately led to writing this book you now hold in your hands. The tools and exercises here reflect my experience from both sides of the couch.

Disclaimer

Truth be told, a book cannot replace human interaction. A book is not therapy. A book can't help you in crisis, hug you when you're sad, or bring you soup when you're sick. Books can't create the relational magic required for emotional healing. But books *can* be a lifeline when you're stuck, alone, and spinning out of control. That's how it was for me. I wrote this book because it was the one my younger self needed, when she possessed neither the skill nor the energy to sort through the mountain of available information.

Who This Book Is For

If you've ever looked at the prompts at the end of a chapter or skimmed over the suggested exercises and thought, *Nope*, this book is for you. Even short exercises can take too much time and bandwidth when you're feeling overwhelmed. The inability to "do the work" is not a personal failing or character flaw—it's a reality that is both understandable and fixable, assuming you are in a safe enough environment with choices and access to resources.

The Getting Unstuck Workbook is presented in a *Choose Your Own Adventure* format; you can jump around in any order you want and do not need to start at the beginning or read this book sequentially. Feel free to skip around and take as many breaks as you need. Each part of this book includes an assortment of activities, including charts, exercises, fill-in-the-blank sections, journal prompts, challenges, rituals, and suggested resources. Not everyone responds to the same types of tasks, so I created the following quiz to help you tailor the work to your specific self-help style.

Quiz: What's Your Self-Help Style?

Instructions: Read the following ten questions, and circle the answer that best represents you for each question. Don't think too hard; choose whichever answer jumps out at you first. If you're stuck between two answers, circle them both.

1. If you have a problem, which of these are you most likely to do?
   A. Think about why the problem exists
   B. Journal about the problem
   C. Take an action about the problem
   D. Pause and reflect on your choices

2. Which of these self-care strategies would you pick if you were overwhelmed?
   A. Make a to-do list
   B. Listen to music
   C. Reach out to a trusted friend
   D. Take a yoga or meditation class

3. Which of these date-night activities sound the most fun?
   A. Playing board games and getting a pizza
   B. Going to the restaurant where you first met your partner
   C. Attending a costume party
   D. Getting a couples' massage

4. You're on a plane, and you can watch only one of these films. Which do you choose?

   A. *Inception*

   B. *The Notebook*

   C. *The Avengers*

   D. *My Octopus Teacher*

5. If you were a food, which of these would you choose to be?

   A. Soufflé

   B. Chocolate-covered strawberry

   C. Cheeseburger

   D. Lobster

6. If you were stranded on an island and could have only one of these books to read, which would you choose?

   A. *A Brief History of Time* by Stephen Hawking

   B. *Gone with the Wind* by Margaret Mitchell

   C. *The Lord of the Rings* by J. R. R. Tolkien

   D. *The Power of Now* by Eckhart Tolle

7. You have one free hour this week. Which of these activities would you choose to do in that hour?

   A. Put together a puzzle

   B. Have coffee with a friend

   C. Catch up on work

   D. Hike

8. Assuming you could do any of these easily, which type of movement sounds the most appealing?

   A. Mountain climbing

   B. Ballroom dancing

   C. Surfing

   D. Scuba diving

9. Which animal resonates most with you?
   A. Monkey
   B. Dog
   C. Squirrel
   D. Dolphin

10. After resolving an argument with a friend, which of these would you most want to do with them next?
    A. Talk
    B. Hug
    C. Walk
    D. Cook

Scoring

Instructions: Read the explanations below, and circle whichever icon matches your answers. If you tied, circle both.

If you answered mostly A's, your self-help style is ***thinking***.
Your icon is a thought bubble.

If you see a thought bubble icon in this workbook, that means the exercise is cognitive/thinking based. You won't need to dive into your feelings, take deep breaths, or leave the house to get these tasks done.

If you answered mostly B's, your self-help style is *feeling*.
Your icon is a heart.

If you see a heart icon, that means the exercise is feelings based. You won't need to make lists, strategize, or do any heavy lifting to get these tasks done.

If you answered mostly C's, your self-help style is *doing*.
Your icon is a footprint.

If you see a footprint icon, that means the exercise is doing based. You won't need to feel feelings or think about your life to get these tasks done; footprint exercises are action oriented.

If you answered mostly D's, your self-help style is *being*.
Your icon is a lotus.

If you see a lotus icon, that means the exercise is based on principles of mindfulness.

How to Use This Book

If you're in a rush, skip over all the tasks that don't match your self-help style and only focus on the ones marked with your specific icon. If you have time to explore, consider trying different types of tasks. If you're primarily a feelings-based person but want to try an action-oriented task, look for the footprints. If you're primarily a thinker but want to try a feelings-based task, look for the hearts. To quickly get to the type of work you want to do, use the icons as your GPS.

Key Points and Check-Ins

In addition to the self-help style icons, you'll also encounter a key and a cup.

The key icon highlights the most important points. If you don't want to read through a section, you can jump straight to the key points to save yourself time and energy.

The cup icon indicates a check-in point. The check-ins allow you to pause, absorb the material, and regroup. Like a coffee date with a good friend, the check-ins will help you stay accountable to yourself.

Daily Practice

Patterns and habits are like a five-lane superhighway in your brain, and building new pathways is like whacking your way through an overgrown forest. If you don't want your brain to default to the superhighway, you'll likely need a daily practice. The problem with most daily practices is that they ask *way* too much of our brains. Even journaling a single page or taking a ten-minute walk can feel impossible after a stressful day or a restless night. The daily practice in this book takes less than one minute and is simply this:

> **Evening practice:** Pick two things.
> **Morning practice:** Make your bed.

I'll explain.

Evening Practice

For the evening practice, all you need to do is jot down two quick notes. It's better to write it on paper, or in your journal, as opposed to typing it in your phone's Notes app or in a Word doc on your computer.

1. Write down one *good* thing that happened during the day. This could be an event, it could be hitting all the green lights on your way to work, or it could be when someone smiled at you or let you merge into traffic. If your entire day was a disaster, your one thing could be that you ended the day with breath in your lungs.

2. Write down one *realistic* thing you want to get done the next day. Keep it small enough that you'll do it. You might not be able to make giant changes, but maybe you can empty the dishwasher, knock one quick errand off your list, or return an email you've been avoiding. You likely have a mile-long to-do list, and you can certainly do as many tasks as you want, but for your daily evening practice, just pick *one*.

Morning Practice

For the morning practice, make your bed (or your side of the bed) *as soon as you get up*. Even if the rest of the room is a disaster, even if you haven't showered in days, even if the kids are bouncing off the walls, take a few seconds to make your bed. And don't worry about trying to execute a Pinterest-worthy, multilayered, many-throw-pillow situation. Just smooth out the sheets and fold over the blanket.

That's it.

Why should you bother with this daily practice?

When it comes to building strength in the gym, building intimacy in a relationship, or building new habits for yourself, it's more important to develop *consistency* than *intensity*. As *Atomic Habits* author James Clear put it, "Intensity makes a good story. Consistency makes progress." Making your bed starts the day with the message, "You are worth taking care of." Writing down one good thing in the evening helps power down your brain so you can get to sleep. Writing down one small task you want to accomplish primes your brain to do it the next day.

A Note Before We Start

The change process can be painful and slow, and there will be times when you might want to throw this book across the room. Stay the course. Even if you feel like an imposter, even if you feel like a hollow shell of a person, even if you worry that you have nothing to offer the world, I can promise you this: at the bottom of the self-exploration ocean, you will find someone worth the effort. As mind and lifestyle coach Hiral Nagda put it, "Peel yourself layer by layer. There is an absolute earth-shattering magnificent person waiting to be discovered."

You may feel lonely and disconnected. You may feel like you're tumbling about with no sense of what to do or which way is up. You may feel overwhelmed trying to assemble the fragmented puzzle pieces of your life. All those feelings make sense. But remember these three things:

1. **You are not crazy.** Even your most baffling symptoms make sense in context.
2. **You are not broken.** Your brain, mind, and heart may get injured, but you are unbreakable.
3. **You are not hopeless.** *Dum spiro spero* is a Latin phrase that means, "As long as I breathe, I hope." If you are still breathing, there is still hope.

Let's begin.

The
Getting *Unstuck*
Workbook

PART 1

Cracking the Procrastination Code

How to Break Bad Habits

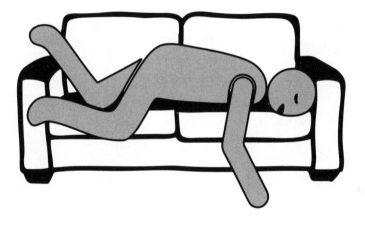

This section blasts through the myths that keep you stuck between knowing what you *want* to do and what you *actually* do. You'll get the key to overcoming procrastination, a set of power tools to manage anxiety, and a road map to get yourself unstuck.

Bad habits repeat themselves again and again, not because you don't want to change but because you have the wrong system for change . . . you do not rise to the level of your goals, you fall to the level of your systems.

—James Clear, *Atomic Habits*

H ave you ever sat on the couch eating snacks and binge-watching Netflix instead of going to the gym (which you promised yourself you'd start doing)? Who among us hasn't had the frustrating experience of knowing exactly what we needed to do to feel better, solve a problem, or reach a goal, but nevertheless doing the exact opposite? My hunch is that you can relate to the feeling of *not* doing the things you know will get you moving and *often* doing the things you know will keep you stuck. No shame. We all do this. There's even a name for it in the academic world—it's called the *intention-action gap.**

⚷ Put simply, the intention action gap is this:

my good intention

The Sea of Stuck

my successful outcome

💭 Mind the Gap

Instructions: Fill in the chart with your good intentions and current outcomes. On the left, list the top six things you want (good health, financial abundance, happy relationships, etc.), and on the right, write down the status of these goals. Do not shame yourself if your status column says "Unfinished" or "Haven't started." That's what this workbook is for.

---

*The theory of reasoned action (TRA) and the theory of planned behavior (TPB) rest on the assumption that behaviors are best predicted by intentions. The TRA was developed by Martin Fishbein and Icek Ajzen in the late 1960s.

my good
intention

The Sea
of Stuck

my successful
outcome

As a therapist, I often see people after they've fallen into the "sea of stuck." The stories I hear usually sound like this:

- "I'm just so lazy."
- "I'm such a procrastinator."
- "I don't know what's wrong with me."
- "My brain hates me."
- "I struggle with motivation."

💭 What Are Your Stuck Stories?

Instructions: Write down the reasons you fall into the sea of stuck. Circle Y for yes or N for no as appropriate if it's possible there's another explanation besides the story you tell yourself.

My Story About Why I'm Stuck	Could This Be Wrong?
	Y/N
	Y/N
	Y/N
	Y/N
	Y/N

Laziness and lack of motivation are *not* the reasons you fall into the sea of stuck. What's the *real* story behind all those unmet goals, abandoned to-do lists, and unread books?

🔑 **One big reason you might be stuck (assuming you're in a safe environment with access to resources and not contending with chronic medical conditions or other contributing factors) is because you haven't built a bridge to cross the intention-action gap.**

Building Your Bridge

You can try to cross a canyon on a single strand of rope, but the rope likely will fray and break under the strain. Many people experience the same phenomenon when they try to cross the intention-action gap using willpower and positive thinking alone.

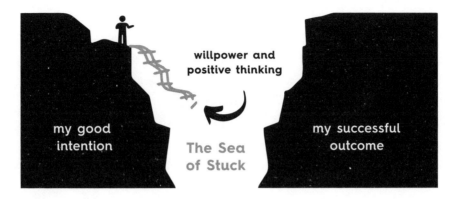

A single strand of rope is easily broken. But a rope bridge made of interwoven strands is way less likely to collapse. To successfully journey across the intention-action gap, you'll interweave multiple approaches. I call this process the Four S's of Bridge Building:

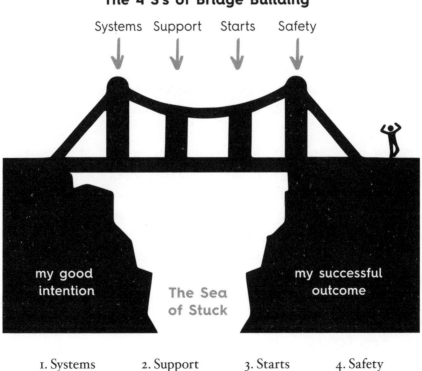

1. Systems   2. Support   3. Starts   4. Safety

Systems

Did you ever learn that it's good to set goals? If you're like most people, the answer is yes. Did you ever learn that it's *not* good to set goals? If you're like most people, the answer is no. When you zoom focus on goals, it's easy to forget that every successfully achieved goal required a *system* to make it possible. A scroll through any social media site will yield millions of videos/photos/tweets of successful outcomes. We all compare our first mile to someone else's finish-line celebration. But you'll almost never see people celebrating the system that *created* the successful outcome. The first S of your intention-action bridge is *systems*.

Atomic Habits author James Clear identifies the difference between goals and systems. He writes [italics mine], "If you're a coach, your *goal* is to win a championship. Your *system* is what your team does at practice each day. If you're an entrepreneur, your *goal* is to build a million-dollar business. Your *system* is your sales and marketing process." Without a system, a goal is wishful thinking at best and a setup for failure at worst. Sound extreme? A *Forbes* article highlighted a shocking statistic: "Researchers from four top business schools have collaborated to show that in many cases goals do more harm than good."

The problem with goals includes the following:

▸ Dreaming about goals is a way to avoid doing the work of achieving goals.
▸ Creating goals sets you up for all-or-nothing thinking.
▸ Achieving goals only provides temporary satisfaction.

Setting goals is like sitting in a parked car dreaming about your destination. You know you *want* to get somewhere. You can fantasize and visualize what it will be like when you arrive. You can text your friends and tell them you're planning to travel. You can journal and chant affirmations about your destination. But until you put your car in drive and start moving, you're going nowhere. Once you plug your destination into your GPS, you don't think about the destination again. Instead, you focus on the directions. *Where* you want to go is the goal. The directions you take to get there are the *system*. Instead of focusing on goals, you want to focus on *systems*. Systems are one of the four strands that weave together your intention-action gap bridge. To get your systems to stick, remember the acronym SET—**Small**, **Easy**, **Truthful**.

Small

If you haven't left the house in months, a system in which you try to go to a dozen networking events a week and run ten miles a day is unlikely to stick. For your system to succeed, it needs to be small. Ridiculously small. So small you feel a little silly doing it. The smaller the system, the more likely it'll stick.

Easy

If you want to learn piano, it helps to keep the piano somewhere easily accessible. If you stash the piano in a basement that requires you to walk down a set of murder stairs and then wade through piles of storage bins, you're not going to practice. Make your system as easy and convenient as possible. If you want to exercise, put your sneakers near the door. If you want to eat less fast food, stock your fridge with stuff you can easily grab when you're hungry.

Truthful

The first commandment of successful systems is, "Thou shalt not lie to thyself" (Procrastination 24:7). Part 4 of this book discusses self-deception in detail, but for the purposes of creating systems, remember to be honest with yourself about both your willingness to do things *and* the reality of your life stressors. If you live with five children, four dogs, three chickens, and your mother-in-law, it is not truthful to say you'll journal for two hours a day and spend four hours in meditation.

⌐O For systems to be successful, they need to be *small*, *easy*, and *truthful*.

💭 Building Your Systems

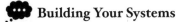

Instructions: Follow these steps.

Step 1: Think about what you want, and write it down in the Goal column of the following chart.

Step 2: Think about the system that will get you there, and write that in the System column. Don't forget to keep your system small, easy, and truthful.

Step 3: Tape a piece of paper over the Goal column so you can't see it at all. Focusing on your goals keeps you stuck. Focusing on your systems gets you moving.

Goal	System (Small, Easy, Truthful)
I want to run a marathon.	Put on my sneakers every morning, and run for two minutes three times a week.
I want to write a book.	Commit to four minutes of writing four times a week even if I don't have anything to say.
I want a better job.	Take one online class each month to build my job skills.

 **Check-In**

Instructions: Either think about the following questions or write about them in your journal.

- ▸ What do you think about setting goals versus creating systems?
- ▸ Where in your past have you set goals but gave up on them? What would have helped make it easier for you to keep going?
- ▸ Review your Systems column. Are your systems all small, easy, and truthful? If not, revise them.
- ▸ How are you doing with your daily practice? If you've started doing the morning and evening tasks, congratulations! If not, consider what system you can create to help you complete them.

Observation: One takeaway from this work is:

_____

Recommendation: Something I can do with this information is:

_____

Support

The second S of the Four S's of Bridge Building is *support*. The idea of seeking support can feel off-putting because it involves other people, and other people often seem scary and inaccessible. Can you white-knuckle your way into doing what you want to do without *any* support? Possibly. Is it likely that you're going to succeed? Doubtful. Fortunately, "support" doesn't always need to include other people. If you've spent years isolated and alone, being told to "just ask for help" is unrealistic and a setup for a shame spiral. This section discusses four different types of support, but only one requires actual human interaction. The four types of support (in increasing order of difficulty) are solo, viewer, virtual, and in-person.

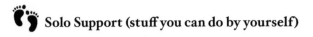 **Solo Support (stuff you can do by yourself)**

Instructions: Follow the steps below.

Step 1: Create a list of songs, movies, or videos that you can listen to or watch when you need an extra dose of "I can do this." You can use the spaces below, write them down in your journal, or create playlists on your phone or computer.

_____

_____

_____

_____

_____

Step 2: Make a list of all the "you got this" energy boosters that you can do by yourself. Examples include taking a cold shower, doing twenty-five jumping jacks, eating something super spicy, or giving yourself a pep talk. Use the spaces below, or write them down in your journal.

_____

_____

_____

_____

_____

Step 3: Using everything you wrote from steps 1 and 2, complete the following chart. The best time to deploy a solo support is right before you talk yourself out of doing what you want to do. See the examples to get started.

My Solo Support	The Best Time to Use It
My "Let's Get out of Bed and DOOOO THIS" playlist	First thing in the morning *before* I start scrolling on my phone and end up in bed for another hour
YouTube video with the training montage from my favorite sports movie	Right before I talk myself out of putting on my sneakers and getting out the door to the gym

👣 Viewer Support (listening to or watching people interact online without participating)

You don't need to talk to anyone to benefit from the support of online communities. Read their posts, listen to their conversations, and watch what they do. Disclaimer: Viewer support is not appropriate if one of the community requirements is for all members to participate or if it is a closed group that does not permit lurkers.

Instructions: Follow the steps below.

Step 1: Look for online resources (websites, message boards, online communities, etc.) that focus on whatever challenge you're facing.

Step 2: Fill in the spaces below.

FIVE WEBSITES THAT COULD BE GOOD POSSIBILITIES FOR VIEWER SUPPORT INCLUDE THE FOLLOWING:

1. _____

2. _____

3. _____

4. _____

5. _____

Step 3: Circle whichever online community you are going to try first. Then, fill in the spaces below:

The website I'm going to try first is _____.

Things I like about this online community include _____
_____.

Things I don't like about this online community include _____
_____.

Step 4: Do I like this community enough to utilize it? (circle one) Y/N

If you circled Y, skip step 5. If you circled N, continue to step 5.

Step 5: Circle whichever online community you're going to try next. Then repeat steps 3 and 4. Continue doing this until you've found an online community that will work for your viewer support needs.

👣 Virtual Support (online or phone interactions)

Going to "group support" used to require you to drive to a new place, get out of the car, walk into a room you've never seen, and talk to people you've never met. *Shudder.* Thankfully, you no longer need to plunge headfirst into the deep end of the human interaction pool. You can safely dip your toes in through virtual micro-connections.

Instructions: You have lots of choices for how to participate with virtual communities. You can comment on a post, DM a group member, chime in during an online forum, speak during a group phone meeting, or turn on your camera during a Zoom. Pick a group, and go.

👣 In-Person Support (the only one in which full-length people are involved)

Seeking real-life support can feel daunting, but the rewards far outweigh the risk. Although solo, viewer, and virtual support is better than no support at all, face-to-face interaction is the most powerful.

Instructions: Follow the steps below.

Step 1: Put a check mark next to any of the following options you're willing to consider trying. Cross out any that are irrelevant to you. (If you don't have a dog, for example, cross out the dog park option.)

Step 2: For the options that you are willing to consider trying, write in the spaces below what you need to do to make it happen and then write one resource (a website, a person you know, or anything you can use to help you make it happen).

Step 3: Pick *one* of the options that you checked. Draw a big circle around it. Commit to getting started with it within the next three days.

▸ Reach out to people I already know _____

    To make this happen, I need to _____.

    One resource that might help is _____.

▸ Volunteer _____

    To make this happen, I need to _____.

    One resource that might help is _____.

▸ Join a community activity _____

    To make this happen, I need to _____.

    One resource that might help is _____.

▸ Go to a professional organization meeting _____

    To make this happen, I need to _____.

    One resource that might help is _____.

▸ Go to a dog park _____

    To make this happen, I need to _____.

    One resource that might help is _____.

▸ Go to an in-person support group meeting _____

    To make this happen, I need to _____.

    One resource that might help is _____.

▸ Join a book club _____

    To make this happen, I need to _____.

One resource that might help is _____.

▸ Attend a religious service _____

   To make this happen, I need to _____.

   One resource that might help is _____.

▸ Attend a game night _____

   To make this happen, I need to _____.

   One resource that might help is _____.

▸ Take a fitness class _____

   To make this happen, I need to _____.

   One resource that might help is _____.

▸ Take a community class _____

   To make this happen, I need to _____.

   One resource that might help is _____.

▸ Look at meetup.com or a similar site for real-life events _____

   To make this happen, I need to _____.

   One resource that might help is _____.

▸ Shop at a local store and talk to the people who work there _____

   To make this happen, I need to _____.

   One resource that might help is _____.

▸ Join a local political advocacy group _____

   To make this happen, I need to _____.

   One resource that might help is _____.

▸ Go to a therapist or coach (in-person) _____

   To make this happen, I need to _____.

   One resource that might help is _____.

☕ Check-In

Instructions: Either think about the following questions or write about them in your journal.

- ▸ Which supports did you find easiest to try? Which were the most challenging?
- ▸ If you skipped the support section altogether, consider revisiting it and attempting one of the exercises.
- ▸ What surprised you most about doing this section?
- ▸ How are you doing with your daily practice?

Observation: One takeaway from this work is:

_____

Recommendation: Something I can do with this information is:

_____

Starts

You can create a perfectly engineered system, design a flawless support plan, and fill your day planner with motivational stickers, but if you don't start, you won't move. The pressure to cross the finish line can render you frozen at the starting gate—especially in a culture that puts a high value on completion. You don't see people handing out medals at the beginning of a race. But as Becky Blades, author of *Start More Than You Can Finish*, put it, "Clichés that say finishing is everything and that a start without a finish is a moral failure—they don't do the job they intended. Likely, these tropes don't make us *finish more*, they just make us *start less* . . . placing guardrails around initiative is the opposite of encouragement. It douses creative courage and stunts our growth. And it matters. We need to start more." Mucky starts, clunky starts, awkward starts—it doesn't matter. The only way to mess up a start is to not start at all.

 **Getting Started**

Instructions: Follow the steps below.

Step 1: On a new piece of paper, write the top ten reasons why you think you can't do what you want to do. Maybe you tell yourself you don't have what it takes, that you don't have enough time, or that you aren't smart enough.

Step 2: Either tear up the piece of paper and throw it away or burn it, and then move on to the next exercise.

 **Starting Strategies**

Instructions: Follow the steps below.

Step 1: Look at the table on the next page. The first column holds a starting strategy, and the second column explains how to use it. Use the table here or copy it into your journal or notebook.

Step 2: Highlight or circle which starting strategy you're going to try first.

Step 3: Try it. Shoot for three days, then five, then a week, and then try it for three weeks.

Step 4: Write down your results.

Step 5: Go back to step 2 and repeat.

Starting Strategy	How to Use It	Did I Try It?	Results
Thirty-second rule	Whatever the thing is you want to do, commit to doing it for just thirty seconds, and then you can stop if you don't want to keep going. Set a timer. If you want to stop after thirty seconds, do not beat yourself up. Try again the next day.	Y/N	
Just get dressed	Don't worry about actually doing the thing; get dressed as if you were going to do it. If you want to go the gym, put on your gym clothes. If you want to meet people, get dressed as if you were going out. Do not beat yourself up if you don't finish. This is a starting strategy, and with enough repetition, you'll eventually get out the door.	Y/N	
Just drive there	Drive to wherever you want to go. Wait in the parking lot for five minutes and then give yourself full permission to leave.	Y/N	
Tell someone your plan	Find someone with whom you can check in before and after you do a thing. This will help keep you accountable to yourself.	Y/N	
Bribe yourself	Make a deal with yourself that if you do X, you get to have Y.	Y/N	
Procrastinate by doing something you hate	Nothing will get you more excited to do the thing you're avoiding than doing something else you don't want to do. So if you're not going to finish updating your résumé, at least your toilet will get scrubbed.	Y/N	

Starting Strategy	How to Use It	Did I Try It?	Results
Just do what's next	Looking at all the steps you need to take can make getting started feel impossible. On a sticky note, write down *only* the next step in your process. Then do it.	Y/N	
Don't start at the beginning	You can trick your brain into action by starting in the middle of a project instead of at the beginning. If you want to write a novel, don't start with the intro. If your goal is to read a self-help book, open to a random page and start there. If you want to design a website, don't start with the home page. Start anywhere in the process except the beginning.	Y/N	

From Stuck to Start: The OODA Loop

Fighter pilots are trained to make split-second decisions and take decisive and immediate action. In the 1950s, Colonel John Boyd, a US Air Force fighter pilot, Pentagon consultant, and military strategist, created a model called the OODA loop—Observe, Orient, Decide, Act.* The OODA loop is a highly effective strategy for getting from *stuck* to *start*.

❀ Work Your OODA Loop

Instructions: Each component of the OODA loop (observe, orient, decide, act) is described in the following chart. The next time you struggle to get started, use this chart to create your own OODA loop, and write down your experience in the Notes column.

---

* Boyd's OODA loop is a complex military strategy that's been heavily modified here. Variations of the OODA loop are often used in the litigation and business worlds to improve decision-making skills.

OODA Component	How to Do It	Notes
Observe	Notice your impulse to procrastinate, avoid, or not start the thing you're wanting to start. Observe the thoughts you're thinking and the stories or excuses you're tempted to tell yourself.	
Orient	Notice your body sensations, and describe them (out loud). Where in your body do you notice tension? What is your heart rate? What do your legs and arms feel like?	
Decide	Make a list of three choices available to you right now. In this moment. Not after you buy the gear, not after the next episode of your show . . . now. If your choices all feel too big, make them small enough until at least one of them is a doable micro-yes.	
Act	Pick the easiest micro-yes on your list, and do it. Repeat the process.	

Is getting started hard? Yes. But it is often equally hard to stay stuck. In the book *Alcoholics Anonymous* (known as the "Big Book" among those in the program), the authors write: "We thought we could find an easier, softer way. But we could not. With all the earnestness at our command, we beg of you to be fearless and thorough from the very start."

We often stay stuck because we believe there's an easy way and a hard way, and our brains are inclined to do what *appears* easy. But "easy" is a myth. A phrase heard often in the wellness world is "Choose your hard."*

It's hard to go to the gym after months of inertia. But it's also hard to feel sluggish and unwell.

Choose your hard.

It's hard to look at your finances when you've avoided them for years. But it's also hard to be in debt and to not know where your money is going.

---

*The original author of the expression "Choose your hard" is unknown.

Choose your hard.

It's hard to meet new people. But it's also hard to feel isolated and disconnected.

Choose your hard.

It's hard to clean your space when you've neglected it for months. But it's also hard to live in clutter and chaos.

Choose your hard.

It's hard to break habits and stop doing things you're used to doing. But it's also hard to continue participating in behaviors that are harmful to your well-being.

Choose your hard.

⚷ A big disclaimer about the "Choose your hard" philosophy:

You can choose your hard only when you have choices. You cannot choose your hard in situations of oppression, systemic racism, or power differentials, when choices are not available.

☕ Check-In

Instructions: Either think about the following questions or write about them in your journal.

- ▸ Have you started? If not, go back to the Starts section, pick a strategy, and use it.
- ▸ What are your fears about starting? What are your fears about finishing?
- ▸ Did you work your OODA loop? How did it go?
- ▸ Are you telling yourself it's easier not to do things than to do things? How true is that?
- ▸ How are you doing with your daily practice?

Observation: One takeaway from this work is:

_____

Recommendation: Something I can do with this information is:

_____

Safety

The final S in the Four S's of Bridge Building—the key to crossing the intention-action gap once and for all—is *safety*.

What does that mean?

A brain that feels safe rarely falls into the sea of stuck. When your brain decides a situation is unsafe, it will shift out of logic mode into survival mode—aka fight, flight, and freeze.*

Fight	Flight	Freeze
Can feel like huge emotional reactions, irritability, restlessness, edginess, and picking fights.	Can feel like panic, hypervigilance, avoidance, anxiety, and like you need to get out of a situation immediately.	Can feel like indecisiveness, heaviness, fatigue, and numbness.
Fight is your **sympathetic** nervous system trying to protect you.	Flight is your **sympathetic** nervous system trying to protect you.	Freeze is your **parasympathetic** nervous system trying to protect you.

You might wonder, *Are my brain and my body trying to protect me when clearly I'm safe and there's nothing wrong?*

Fair question.

It may be logically true that you're safe, but if your body disagrees for any reason, it will win every time. You can't *think* your way out of how your body *feels*.

🔑 To manage a fight, flight, or freeze response, you need to learn a different language than logic.

You probably were taught to change your *mind* if you wanted to change your *mood*. The field of cognitive behavioral therapy (CBT) is based on the idea that your thoughts create

---

*There is a fourth survival response called the fawn response, or "people-pleasing response." If you struggle with people-pleasing, you can check out the codependency exercises in part 3.

your feelings. Sometimes this is true, but CBT has one major flaw: it completely ignores the fact that you live in a body. You can't separate your mind from your body (unless you ingest certain types of psychedelics, which is an entirely different topic). Everything in your body impacts your mind and your mood. Anxiety, depression, and mood swings are *not* "all in your head." Mental health is not solely in your mind.

⚷ Mental health is not a mental process; mental health is a physiological process.

You are a biological organism with a nervous system. Your nervous system automatically scans and evaluates your environment and makes split-second decisions without your input. Knowing how your nervous system works—and how to drive it—is the secret to cracking the procrastination code.

Your Nervous System

Sympathetic	Parasympathetic
Pupils Dilated	Pupils Constricted
Increased Saliva	Decreased Saliva
Faster Heart Rate	Slower Heart Rate
Inhibited Digestion	Stimulated Digestion

Your nervous system has multiple branches, including the parasympathetic nervous system (PNS) and the sympathetic nervous system (SNS). You are not supposed to stay permanently planted in either the SNS or the PNS. Humans aren't designed to always feel energized or always feel calm.

🔑 The goal is to have a *dynamic* nervous system that smoothly transitions like a seesaw between SNS and PNS.

What It's SUPPOSED to Look Like: Dynamic

Rest / Activity
Peaceful / Excited
Calm / Energized
Self-Care / Care of Others
Relaxation / Productivity

Parasympathetic Nervous System

Your PNS is the brake pedal of your body—it is responsible for slowing you down. You need your parasympathetic nervous system to quiet your mind, slow your heart rate, and digest your food. When your PNS decides something might harm you, it sounds the alarm and says, "DANGER! SHUT DOWN THE SYSTEM!" When you get stuck in parasympathetic shutdown, it feels like this:

Dorsal Vagal Shutdown: STUCK on DOWN

Procrastination
Exhaustion
No Motivation
Depression

Any Perceived Threat

If your brain is stuck in a parasympathetic response—often referred to as a dorsal vagal shutdown—you're not going to be able to make decisions or take actions, and you won't feel inspired to do much of anything. Many people attribute parasympathetic responses to laziness. But the word *lazy* is a moral judgment, not a biological reality.

🔑 **The PNS shutdown response (aka "freeze") has nothing to do with laziness or character.**

Sympathetic Nervous System

Your SNS is the gas pedal of your body—it is responsible for your "get up and go" energy. (If you get sympathetic and parasympathetic confused, remember that *para*sympathetic sounds like *para*chute, and a parachute brings you down.) When you get stuck in an overactive sympathetic response, it feels like this:

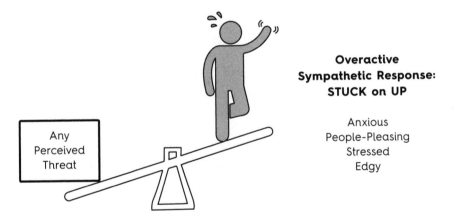

Overactive Sympathetic Response: STUCK on UP

Anxious
People-Pleasing
Stressed
Edgy

Any Perceived Threat

The Two Types of Procrastination

Procrastination is a fancy way to say, "I tried to cross the intention-action gap but fell into the sea of stuck." Many people learned to believe that procrastination is a mindset issue.

Although mindset certainly plays a role, procrastination is first and foremost a *nervous system response*, not a character defect. If your brain feels unsafe because of stress, overwhelm, trauma, or burnout, the decision-making and action-taking parts of your brain go offline* and survival physiology kicks into action.

🔑 **Procrastination is a sign that your nervous system has shifted into survival mode.**

You may think of procrastination as a singular thing, the act of not doing what you should be doing, but because your nervous system can get stuck in two directions, there are two types of procrastination:

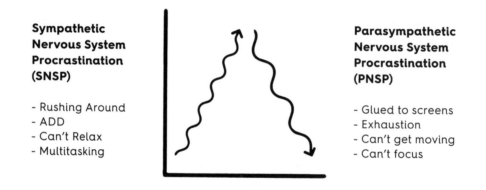

Sympathetic Nervous System Procrastination (SNSP)

- Rushing Around
- ADD
- Can't Relax
- Multitasking

Parasympathetic Nervous System Procrastination (PNSP)

- Glued to screens
- Exhaustion
- Can't get moving
- Can't focus

When some people hear that procrastination is a physiological response, they often object with a snarky, "So you're saying it's totally fine to do nothing because procrastination is a nervous system response?"

No.

Knowing that procrastination is a nervous system response doesn't excuse inertia; it explains it. Accurately describing a problem is the first step to solving the problem. Sympathetic nervous system procrastination (SNSP) requires a different set of tools than parasympathetic nervous system procrastination (PNSP), and neither requires shame, willpower,

---

*"Offline" is a metaphor. Your brain is not simple and cannot be reduced to switches, wires, and light bulbs.

or positive thinking. If you're stuck in SNSP, the solution is to *down-regulate*. If you're stuck in PNSP, the solution is to *up-regulate*. The next section shows you how to do both.

❋ Where Do You Get Stuck?

Instructions: Follow the steps below.

Step 1: Look at the table below. Highlight or circle any of the symptoms you regularly experience. Disclaimer: Always check with a medical doctor to rule out medical causes before assuming a symptom has emotional or psychological origins.

Stuck on "On" (SNS)	Stuck on "Off" (PNS)
Difficulty making decisions	Fatigue
Anxiety/panic	Struggle to take actions
Insomnia	Brain fog
Agitated	Feelings of heaviness
Racing heart	Sluggish
Lack of focus	Feel frozen
Can't relax	Overwhelmed
Digestive issues	Hopelessness
Jumpy	Numbness/dissociation
Muscle tension	Avoidance
Easily angered	Shame
Lack of appetite	Using food for comfort
Racing mind	Procrastination

Step 2: Do you struggle more with feeling stuck on "on," stuck on "off," or equally stuck between both? (circle one) ON/OFF/BOTH

Step 3: Fill in the blanks (either write your answers here or copy them into a notebook or journal):

The situations when I usually feel stuck on "on" include:

_____

_____

_____

_____

The situations when I usually feel stuck on "off" include:

_____

_____

_____

_____

The people (or types of people) who make my nervous system feel stuck on "on" include:

_____

_____

_____

_____

The people (or types of people) who make my nervous system feel stuck on "off" include:

_____

_____

_____

_____

To create a sense of safety in your body, you can try the following exercises. The first set is designed to help you down-regulate when you feel stuck in the "on" (SNS) direction, and the second set can help you up-regulate when you feel stuck on "off" (PNS). Some of the techniques work for both responses, and you may be surprised by which techniques work for you and which ones don't. Experiment with as many as possible to see which resonate with your nervous system.

✿ How to Help Your Body Down-Regulate: Stuck on "On" (SNS)

Instructions: The following techniques can help your nervous system slow down.

Step 1: Before you start, notice what sensations you're feeling in your body.

Step 2: Pick one, two, or all of the following techniques, and write where or when you are most likely to try it.

Step 3: Try it.

Step 4: Notice what sensations you feel in your body after you try one of the techniques, and log the results in the Results column.

Remember, all the nervous system exercises in the world will not make an unsafe situation safer. These exercises are designed to help your brain access safety when you are, in fact, safe.

Down-Regulation Technique	How to Do It	Best Place/Time to Try This	Did I Try This?	Results
Vocalizing	Sing, hum, or chant "Om." Anytime you vibrate your vocal cords, you signal to your brain that you're not about to be eaten by a lion. This will feel silly. Do it anyway.	This is a great one to do in your car on your way to and/or going home from a stressful situation.	Y/N	
Gargling	Grab some water, gargle it, and make as much noise as you can. For maximum impact, go outside and spit.		Y/N	

Down-Regulation Technique	How to Do It	Best Place/Time to Try This	Did I Try This?	Results
Stretching	Slowly and gently stretch your arms and your legs, one at a time.		Y/N	
Creativity	Grab a coloring book, finger paints, watercolors, or pens, and color, paint, or doodle. This isn't high art. Feel free to make a mess.		Y/N	
Cold	Cold signals safety to your brain. Take a cold shower or a cold bath, hold an ice pack to your neck, or squeeze ice cubes in your hand.		Y/N	
Laughter	Watch silly videos online or watch your favorite stand-up comic, and even if you don't feel like it, laugh anyway.		Y/N	
Foot squeezing	With your consent and the consent of a willing partner, have them hold your feet, sit on your feet, or stand gently on your feet. This can help your brain feel anchored and grounded.		Y/N	
Making eye contact	Set a timer and make eye contact with someone you trust for two minutes. Bonus if you both start laughing.		Y/N	
Arm pushing	Find a sturdy wall and push on it with your hands as hard as you can for thirty seconds (set a timer). Release and notice your body sensations for thirty seconds. Repeat three times.		Y/N	

Down-Regulation Technique	How to Do It	Best Place/Time to Try This	Did I Try This?	Results
Playing catch or juggling	Playing catch creates bilateral (both sides) stimulation in your brain. If you don't have someone available to play catch with, juggling (two or three balls or scarves) is also an option.		Y/N	
Lying down	Lying on the floor (or even better, in the grass) helps your brain locate your body in space. This is a safety signal that slows your fight-or-flight response.		Y/N	
Weighted blanket	Lie down under a weighted blanket. If weighted blankets make you feel claustrophobic, you can hold a weighted pillow on your lap or put a sock full of rice on your neck.		Y/N	
Eye gazing	Sitting up straight, let your eyes gaze all the way to the left without turning your head. Hold that position, and count to fifteen. Then let your eyes gaze all the way to the right. Hold and count to fifteen. Look up, hold, and count to fifteen and then look down, hold, and count to fifteen. Repeat two times on all sides.		Y/N	

🪷 How to Help Your Body Up-Regulate: Stuck on "Off" (PNS)

Instructions: The following techniques can help your nervous system come out of freeze.

Step 1: Before you start, notice what sensations you're feeling in your body.

Step 2: Pick one, two, or all of the following techniques, and write where or when you are most likely to try it.

Step 3: Try it.

Step 4: Notice what sensations you feel in your body after you try one of the techniques, and log the results in the Results column.

Remember, these exercises are not intended to "cure" anything. They are intended to help move you out of a shutdown state into a more mobilized state.

Up-Regulation Technique	How to Do It	Situation Where It Could Be Helpful	Will I Try This?	Results
Minimal stimulation	Close your screens, turn off your music, and find a quiet place. Notice how your body responds to the quiet.		Y/N	
Soft light	Light candles, put a colored light bulb in a lamp, use a salt lamp, or string up twinkle lights to create a softly lit room. Notice how your body reacts.		Y/N	
Stretching	Gently, one part at a time, stretch your arms, legs, back, shoulders, and neck. Notice your body sensations as you do this.		Y/N	

Up-Regulation Technique	How to Do It	Situation Where It Could Be Helpful	Will I Try This?	Results
Soft music	Put on peaceful-sounding instrumental music. Listen for three minutes, and notice your body sensations. Turn off the music for three minutes, and notice your body sensations. Repeat three times.		Y/N	
Heat	Put a hot water bottle on your chest or stomach, sit in a sauna and sweat, or put a hot towel around your feet.		Y/N	
Anger	The opposite of depression isn't happiness—it's anger. Find something in the news or on TV that riles you up. Notice your body sensations. A nervous system that can access anger is a nervous system that's mobile.		Y/N	
Making eye contact	Set a timer and make eye contact with someone you trust for two minutes. Bonus if you both start laughing.		Y/N	
Leg pushing	Lie on your back with your feet on a wall. Push as hard as you can with your feet for thirty seconds (set a timer). Release and notice your body sensations for thirty seconds. Repeat three times.		Y/N	
Playing catch or juggling	Bilateral brain stimulation helps access safety. Either play catch with someone or juggle with two or three balls or scarves.		Y/N	

Up-Regulation Technique	How to Do It	Situation Where It Could Be Helpful	Will I Try This?	Results
Eating sour or spicy food	Assuming you don't have any medical issues that would make this dangerous, eat something super spicy or super sour. Notice your body sensations for thirty seconds (set a timer). Drink milk, or coconut milk if you follow a nondairy diet, to calm down the heat. Notice your body sensations for thirty seconds. Repeat three times.		Y/N	

👣 Climbing the Procrastination Ladder

Instructions: The following exercise helps you break down your tasks into micro-yesses. When you say yes to tiny things, you create momentum. Either use the diagram here or copy this into your notebook or journal.

Step 1: Pick something you want to do but have been procrastinating (either PNSP or SNSP).

Step 2: Break down the task into the smallest possible components. These are your micro-yesses. Put the easiest step at the bottom of the ladder and the most difficult step at the top.

Step 3: Do the step at the bottom of the ladder.

Step 4: Do the next step up on the ladder. Repeat until you reach the top.

Important: If you find yourself struggling or resisting a step, make it smaller. A micro-yes forward is always preferable to a giant step untaken. After you complete a step, check the box to mark it complete.

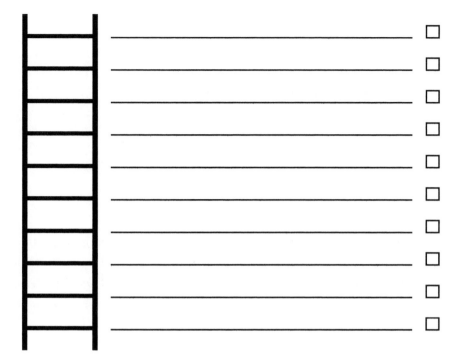

When your brake pedal (PNS) and gas pedal (SNS) are working together smoothly, your nervous system enters a state of *emotional regulation*.

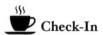 **Check-In**

Instructions: Either think about the following questions or write about them in your journal.

- ▸ What would change if you approached procrastination as a safety issue rather than a laziness issue?
- ▸ What surprised you about the techniques? If you haven't tried them, consider going back to that section and picking one or two to complete.
- ▸ How are you doing with your daily practice?

Observation: One takeaway from this work is:

_____

Recommendation: Something I can do with this information is:

_____

Emotional Regulation

Emotional regulation is a big trend in the wellness world and is hailed as the ultimate sign of healing. Cheeky memes proclaim, "The biggest flex is a regulated nervous system." The zeitgeist now uses *emotional regulation* interchangeably with the word *calm*. But they are not the same. Emotional regulation does *not* require you to feel blissful, grounded, or peaceful.

⊷O **Emotional regulation is not about maintaining a sense of calm. Emotional regulation is about maintaining a sense of *choice*.**

Emotional regulation means that even though you feel uncomfortable, you still can maintain control over your actions and your words.

- You can be regulated *and* angry.
- You can be regulated *and* sad.
- You can be regulated *and* scared.

All feelings are valid, but all *behaviors* are not. Emotional regulation is when you both validate your feelings *and* keep yourself from acting in harmful or suboptimal ways.

⊷O **A big disclaimer about emotional regulation:**

When you feel like nothing you try seems to work, it's easy to blame yourself. Sometimes the wellness world attributes poor outcomes to lack of commitment, lack of effort, or lack of spirituality. But there are no bio-hacks, emotional regulation tricks, or workbook exercises that can make an unsafe situation safe.

🔑 Sometimes when "doing the work" isn't effective, it isn't because you aren't trying hard enough; it's because you aren't *safe* enough.

Your humanity is not as simple as "Hack your brain, heal your life." As the McGill University Office for Science and Society put it, "While science constantly tortures the brain with nuance, the gurus of natural health aim for black-and-white simplicity . . . in an ever-complex world, believing a simple story of good and evil can bring clarity, but this lucidity is a mirage." One of the most pervasive stories of "good and evil" regarding wellness is the idea that anxiety is "bad" and must be cured. But this couldn't be further from the truth. Not only is anxiety not bad, but it is essential for a happy and productive life.

Why You Need Anxiety

I hate feeling anxious as much as you do. It is one of the scarier ways our bodies respond. Anxiety can create feelings of powerlessness, helplessness, paralysis, and shame. You likely were taught to view anxiety as an enemy to overcome or a disease to be cured.

🔑 Anxiety is awful, but it is *not* an attacker or a disease. It is a *response*.

Anxiety—even the kind when you feel like you're about to get squeezed to death by a boa constrictor—is not trying to harm you; it's trying to *help* you. When your car flashes the check engine light, the light is a nuisance, but the light itself is not the problem—the light is a signal pointing *toward* the problem. Anxiety is the check engine light of the mind's dashboard. Anxiety is unpleasant and sometimes it's even debilitating, but it is not the problem. Cutting the wire to your check engine light will turn it off, but the problem inside the engine remains. The check engine light is the symptom; the issue in the engine is the problem. Anxiety is an awful and uncomfortable symptom, but we need it.

Why?

There are four primary functions of anxiety. I call these the "Four P's of Anxiety."

1. **Protect:** Anxiety is a signal from your body that helps *protect* you from dangerous situations.
2. **Prevent:** Anxiety is a cue that can help *prevent* you from showing up unprepared for an event, test, meeting, or situation.
3. **Promote:** Anxiety *promotes* connection. We are evolutionarily wired to bond with other people in anxiety-inducing situations.
4. **Point:** Anxiety is the body's warning system. It *points* toward problems in relationships, dangerous environments, or misalignments with your truth.

♥ **Journal Prompt: The Four P's of Anxiety**

It's easy to think that anxiety "comes out of nowhere" because it often feels like that. But anxiety is the superhero of your story, not the villain. Think about the prompts below, or write about them in your notebook or journal.

1. **Protect:** Think of a time when anxiety (high alertness, hypervigilance, or feeling ready to run) helped *protect* you from a dangerous situation or person.
2. **Prevent:** Think of a time when anxiety *prevented* you from showing up unprepared.
3. **Promote:** Think of a stressful or dangerous situation in which that stress or danger *promoted* everyone around you to be quick to bond with each other, support each other, and engage with each other.
4. **Point:** Think of a time when you ignored your anxiety but later realized it was *pointing* you toward a problem in a job, relationship, or situation.

⚷ **You need anxiety to keep you safe.**

What's the *Real* Problem?

In his thought-provoking book *What's Your Problem?* author Thomas Wedell-Wedellsborg writes: "The way you frame a problem determines which solutions you come up with. By shifting the way you see the problem—that is, by reframing it—you can sometimes find radically better solutions . . . At the heart of this method is a counterintuitive insight: sometimes, to solve a hard problem, *you have to stop looking for solutions to it.*" When it comes to feeling less terrorized by anxiety, you don't need a solution to "cure" it; you need a system to *reframe* it. The next section shows you how.

Reframing Anxiety

When you think there's something inside your brain that's trying to attack you, your brain hears that thought, takes it literally, and immediately shifts into survival mode. As you'll recall from earlier in this part, survival physiology can take the form of stuck on "on" (sympathetic nervous system/gas pedal) or stuck on "off" (parasympathetic nervous system/brake pedal). Anxiety is a function of your sympathetic nervous system, which means the solution is to *down-regulate*. The down-regulation techniques you read about earlier can sometimes be enough on their own, but sometimes anxiety requires a *top-down* strategy before *bottom-up* strategies will work.

What does that mean?

Top-Down Strategies	Bottom-Up Strategies
Top-down strategies are mind (cognitive) based. Mind-based strategies include thinking exercises, troubleshooting, journaling, or analyzing a situation.	Bottom-up strategies are body (somatic) based. Body-based strategies include all of the down- and up-regulation techniques like pushing, pulling, breathing, other movement-based interventions, plus anything using your senses.

Sometimes anxiety can be solved by using only bottom-up strategies. Sometimes it can be solved by using only top-down strategies. More often, anxiety requires a combination of both. The next section gives you top-down tools you can add to your tool-box.

Let's start by first exploring how anxiety manifests in your life.

❀ Getting to Know Your Anxiety

Instructions: Think about how you experience anxiety—the thoughts, emotions, body sensations, and choices you make as a result. Respond to the questions and prompts below.

Physical symptoms: List the physical sensations you feel when you're anxious. Which physical sensations scare you the most?

> [blank response box]

Mental symptoms: List the thoughts you have when you experience anxiety. These might include things like, *I'm having an anxiety attack* or *I'm going to lose control.*

> [blank response box]

Behavioral symptoms: List the people, places, and situations you avoid when you're feeling anxious. List the choices you make to numb or soothe your anxiety.

> [blank response box]

The Problem with Metaphors

Now that you know a little bit more about your anxiety, you can start the *cognitive reframing process*.

⚷ Cognitive reframing is "a process of reconceptualizing a problem by seeing it from a different perspective."*

This section gives you two powerful techniques to reframe anxiety. The first is *metaphor elimination*. Metaphors are great for writing poems, adding color to stories, or describing dreams, but when it comes to anxiety, they are gasoline to a fire. Think about the language most of us use to describe anxiety:

- ▸ I feel like I'm *drowning*.
- ▸ I feel like I'm being *attacked*.
- ▸ I'm *buried* by my anxiety.
- ▸ Everything feels so overwhelming.

Logically, you may know you're speaking in metaphor, but sometimes your brain hears your thoughts and responds as if they're literal. If your brain hears you say, "I'm drowning," it will put you in a state of freeze to help conserve oxygen. If your brain hears you say, "I'm having an anxiety attack," it will think you're literally being attacked and amplify your fight-or-flight response so you can get away safely.

⚷ Changing your language about anxiety makes a huge difference in your ability to manage it.

---

* "Reframing," *APA Dictionary of Psychology*, American Psychological Association, https://dictionary.apa.org/reframing.

💭 Reframing Technique 1: Metaphor Elimination

Instructions: This exercise helps you reframe the language you use about anxiety. Think of what you say when you're anxious, and use the chart below to reframe it with specific and literal language.

Metaphorical Description	Literal Description
I'm drowning.	I feel tightness in my chest, and my stomach is cramping.

To successfully use the next reframing technique, you'll need to first understand the difference between *anxiety*, *fear*, *worry*, and *stress*. Often people use these words interchangeably, but they are not the same.

ANXIETY, FEAR, WORRY, AND STRESS: WHAT'S THE DIFFERENCE?

Term	Definition
Anxiety	Anxiety is a free-floating feeling of unease or dread that's *not* tied to a specific stimulus. Anxiety is a nagging suspicion that "something bad is about to happen" with no logical explanation or imminent threat. Anxiety body sensations can show up as racing thoughts, sweaty palms, dry mouth, tight stomach, and insomnia.

ANXIETY, FEAR, WORRY, AND STRESS: WHAT'S THE DIFFERENCE?

Term	Definition
Fear	Fear produces the same set of body sensations as anxiety, but fear *is* tied to a specific stimulus or imminent threat. If you experience lack of appetite, constant distraction, and sweaty palms when you think you might get fired or wonder if your partner is cheating, that is not anxiety; that is *fear*.
Worry	Worry produces a similar set of body sensations as fear and anxiety but at a much lower intensity. Worry is like diet fear or fear lite. As with fear, worry is tied to a specific stimulus, but it does not feel as intense as fear. You may feel restless, distracted, and jittery about a first date or about getting your kids picked up on time, but if, on a scale of one to ten (with one being the least worried and ten, the most), you are at a six or below, you're experiencing worry, not fear.
Stress	Stress is purely physiological with no specific thoughts attached. If your body feels activated and in "go" mode but you have no specific thoughts that are troubling you, that's pure stress. When stress has a concerning narrative attached to it, it becomes anxiety, fear, or worry.

The next technique helps you distill anxiety (which often feels unmanageable and impossible to navigate) into a worry (which is often more manageable and possible to navigate).

Reframing Technique 2: Turning Anxiety into Worry

Instructions: This exercise helps you turn an anxious thought into a worry. Read through the example and then complete the blank chart, or copy it into your notebook or journal whenever you want to reframe an anxious thought.

Step 1: Write down your anxious thought.

Step 2: Look at your anxious thought, and ask yourself what fear (specific stimulus) is attached to it.

Step 3: Look at your fearful thought, and see if you can pick out specific worries that are attached to the fear.

Step 4: Look at your specific list of worries, and write down your choices for managing the worries.

Anxiety (general thought)	I'm anxious about this trip.
Fear (specific thought)	If I don't get everything ready for this trip, my fear is that we won't be able to go and then my vacation time will be wasted.
Worry (smaller and specific concerns)	I'm worried about getting to the passport office for pictures, getting everything packed, and making sure the kids' teachers know we are going to need their homework assignments ahead of time.
My choices	I can use my lunch hour on Tuesday to go the passport office. I can make sure we pack at least three days ahead of time. I can remind myself that as long as I pack the medication and travel documents, it's okay if I forget to pack socks. I can send an email to the kids' school on Wednesday right after my morning meeting.

Your turn. Fill in the chart below.

Anxiety (general thought)	
Fear (specific thought)	
Worry (smaller and specific concerns)	
My choices	

🔑 **Disclaimer: You almost always can turn anxiety into a fear, but you can't always turn a fear into a worry. If the situation involves safety, a lack of** choices or access to resources, or abuse, fear is a response that matches the situation. This technique is only appropriate if you are in a safe enough environment with access to your basic needs and there is no abuse.

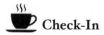 Check-In

Instructions: Either think about the following questions or write about them in your journal.

- ▸ What did you notice as you worked to shift your anxieties into worries?
- ▸ What surprised you about the techniques? If you haven't tried them, consider going back to that section and picking one or two to complete.
- ▸ How are you doing with your daily practice?

Observation: One takeaway from this work is:

_____

Recommendation: Something I can do with this information is:

_____

What About Trauma?

Sometimes, what we think is a "motivation" or "anxiety" problem turns out to be a *trauma* problem. Not every issue, trigger, uncomfortable feeling, or body response is a trauma response. But often, what people call "procrastination" or "lack of motivation" *is* because of trauma. The symptoms mental health practitioners learned to label as a disorder or disease are sometimes the result of neurodivergence and sometimes the result of our brains doing *exactly* what brains are designed to do—go into fight, flight, or freeze in the face of a threat.

It is important as a consumer to know that psychotherapists are not required to be trauma trained or to take any classes about the brain.

🗝 **Before accepting someone *else's* mental health assessment as *your* truth, first ask them (and yourself) if they factored environmental stressors or trauma into their diagnosis.***

What Trauma Is—and Isn't

Think of trauma like digestion. If you eat something your body can't process (for any reason), you are going to experience gastrointestinal distress. If you experience something your brain can't process (for any reason), you are going to experience emotional distress. Digestion is a complex process that happens automatically, without your input. If you eat contaminated food, it's likely you'll get sick, but you also can get sick from eating the same turkey sandwich and chips you've eaten every day for a decade. You don't get to choose when, how, or what will cause your stomach to hurt. Your brain has a similar process when it comes to trauma.

If you experience a horrific event like assault or a natural disaster, the likelihood that your brain will experience trauma is high. You also can experience trauma from things you wouldn't necessarily think of as "traumatic." In Somatic Experiencing (SE), a trauma healing modality pioneered by Dr. Peter Levine, trauma is described as *anything* that's too much, too fast, or too soon for our brains to process. Dr. Levine also adds [italics mine], "Trauma is not what happens *to* us, but what we hold *inside* in the absence of an empathic witness."

The idea that trauma is not defined by the event can be misunderstood and weaponized with toxic positivity statements like, "What happens to you doesn't matter—all that mat-

---

*Diagnoses can be problematic, but they also can bring comfort, relief, and access to insurance coverage and mental health services. Never go off your medication without talking to your doctor.

ters is what you *believe* about what happens to you." This is inaccurate because sometimes life throws things your way that no amount of positive thinking or cognitive reframing will change. To prevent confusion, it is important to know the difference between *trauma, traumatic event, trauma-inducing event,* and *trauma response.*

Term	Definition
Trauma	An internal process during which your brain cannot "digest" an experience.
Traumatic event	Things we can all agree are universally horrific, like rape, assault, oppression, systemic racism, and natural disasters. Traumatic events are always bad, but they do not always cause post-traumatic stress disorder (PTSD) or chronic mental health symptoms.
Trauma-inducing event	Neutral or positive events. Trauma-inducing events are not always "bad" but nevertheless can register in the nervous system as traumatic. Trauma-inducing events can include getting married, having a baby, getting a promotion, moving to a new city, or getting in an argument with your spouse.
Trauma response	Our external expression of internal trauma. Trauma responses can look like panic, depression, anxiety, or any other type of psychological or medical symptom.

Disclaimer: Not all trauma is created equal, and having perspective is important. Perspective allows you to validate your pain and recognize that you have things pretty good. Perspective is useful. Comparing your trauma to someone else's and minimizing your pain as a result is not.

It can be dangerous to attempt deep trauma work without the guidance of a trained professional, so this workbook does not include any intensive trauma-healing exercises. That said, all the nervous system regulation and anxiety techniques listed earlier in this section can be useful and appropriate interventions for trauma. You also can use the next technique and the end-of-level challenge if you need a trauma response intervention.

Don't Start with Why

One of the biggest contributors to feeling stuck with trauma, habits, or anxiety—or any-thing else related to your emotional well-being—is the idea that you need to know why something is happening before you can change it.

This is untrue.

Insight can be useful, and starting with "why" is brilliant as a business principle, but why should never be used as a starting point when you want to change a habit or manage a trauma response.

🔑 **You don't walk up to a burning building and ponder, "I wonder why this building is on fire." You get the people out of the building and ask why later.**

🔑 **You don't need to know *why* you're stuck to get unstuck.**

👣 **Three Steps to Unstuck**

Instructions: Insight and explanation can be helpful, but not at the starting gate. If you're going to ask why questions, wait until *after* you've done the Three Steps to

Unstuck exercise. You can think about these three steps or use your journal or notebook to write them down.

Step 1: Do not ask why you're experiencing a symptom.

Step 2: Ask yourself what are three micro-yesses available to you in this moment that can help you feel a little safer or less alone.

Step 3: Pick a micro-yes from your list, and do it.

╍O Bottom-Line Takeaways

- ▸ To avoid falling into the intention-action gap (aka the sea of stuck), you need a bridge.
- ▸ The four components of your bridge are systems, support, starts, and safety.
- ▸ It's hard to do things. It's also hard *not* to do things. Choose your hard.
- ▸ Mental health is not a mental process; it is a physiological process.
- ▸ Your nervous system has a gas pedal and a brake pedal. You need both.
- ▸ Procrastination is a sign your nervous system has shifted into survival mode.
- ▸ Finding micro-yesses you can do is always preferable to doing nothing.
- ▸ Emotional regulation is not the same as emotional calmness.
- ▸ Symptoms are sometimes the result of brains doing what brains were designed to do.
- ▸ You can experience a horrific event and not have any trauma symptoms, and you can experience trauma symptoms from neutral or even positive events.

DOS AND DON'TS OF BREAKING BAD HABITS

Do	Don't
Build a bridge to cross your intention-action gap.	Assume the reason you can't cross the intention-action gap is because you're lazy—you're not.

DOS AND DON'TS OF BREAKING BAD HABITS

Do	Don't
Remember that the bridge is made of systems, support, starts, and safety.	Try to make your systems too big. Systems should be small, easy, and truthful.
Check in with yourself to see if you're feeling stuck on up mode (sympathetic) or down mode (parasympathetic).	Try to use a "stuck on up" intervention for a "stuck on down" feeling.
Remind yourself that you don't need to know why something is happening to change it.	Ruminate about why you're feeling what you're feeling.

End-of-Level Challenge

As a newbie surfer, you'll quickly learn it is *not* a good idea to try to paddle past big waves. You'll get tumbled hard. Instead, surf instructors teach you to "turtle dive" under the waves when you can't get over them. A turtle dive is when you dive under your board, hold on for dear life, and wait for the wave to pass. You don't gain any ground with turtle dives, but they allow you to hang on until conditions improve.

What a great metaphor for dealing with trauma—or really, for life in general.

Instructions: You will not always have the time, energy, or resources to "paddle forward" past obstacles. During these times, try one of the following five trauma "turtle dives."

Five Ways to Trauma Turtle Dive

1. Conscious dissociation. Let your mind wander, and allow yourself to feel floaty (assuming you can keep yourself safe). You do not have to always stay mindful and present.

2. Consciously use food to comfort yourself (assuming this won't cause a medical emergency).
3. Dive into your favorite show for escape.
4. Let your kids use their screens longer than usual.
5. Take a sick day off work.

O Disclaimer: Trauma turtle dives are not sustainable long-term solutions. Turtle dives in surfing allow you a brief respite before you need to get back on your board and continue paddling. Turtle dives with trauma are designed to give you a little bit of a breather before you need to get back up and continue to move forward.

Congratulations! You've reached the end of this part. Use the space below for final observations and recommendations:

Observations:

_____

_____

_____

Recommendations:

_____

_____

_____

PART 2

Who Are You?

How to Make Friends with Your Mind

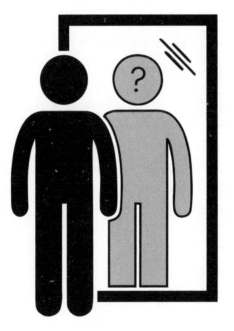

Feeling confused about who you are and what you really want? This part helps you clarify and better understand your likes and dislikes, and it introduces you to different parts of your personality.

Do not let the roles you play in life make you forget who you are.

—Roy T. Bennett

Getting to Know Yourself

You don't need to "fix" yourself—you aren't broken. You might think the goal of inner work is to fix yourself, but it isn't. The goal of any self-help or therapeutic approach isn't to *fix* yourself; it's to *know* yourself beyond the roles you play or the masks you wear. As author Geoffrey Ocaya put it, "Until you know yourself, all that you know is useless, because your life will lack direction." Or as Socrates famously declared, "To know thyself is the beginning of wisdom." He also urged, "My friend . . . care for your psyche . . . know thyself, for once we know ourselves, we may learn how to care for ourselves." Socrates may have said that three to four hundred years before the common era, but that same wisdom would just as easily apply today if he were sitting across from you at the coffee shop, oat milk latte in hand.*

Knowing who you are and what you want is essential to cultivating happiness.

But to know yourself more fully, you also need to come to grips with the good and the bad, the light and the shadow, and the salty and the sour aspects of your personality. Going inside your mind can be a terrifying prospect, which is why so many lives go unexamined and unlived. To do the self-exploration necessary for happiness and wholeness, you'll need to trust that your inner work will not leave you stranded in Shameville. Many people are afraid that if they scratch the surface of their existence, they'll discover they are worthless.

But the opposite is true.

⌐O Refusing to examine what lies beneath the surface doesn't prevent shame; it *amplifies* it.

⌐O Refusing to get curious about your mind doesn't avert pain; it *creates* it.

---

* I see Socrates as an oat milk latte kind of guy and Aristotle as an iced mocha, no whip drinker. Pythagoras probably went for straight espresso, and Plato strikes me as an "I hate coffee. Give me a Red Bull" person.

⌦O Doing self-exploration work doesn't unleash the monster within; it *tames* it.

The question "Who am I?" is one philosophers, scientists, and theologians have wrestled with for millennia. I'm certainly not going to try to shed light on the nature of consciousness or the origin of species here. Instead, we'll start by exploring things about your present-day self—your likes, dislikes, and thought patterns. Then, we'll touch briefly on elements of your past self (no deep dive on past trauma required). You won't need to dwell on your childhood, but as Maya Angelou put it, "You can't really know where you are going until you know where you have been." Next, you'll encounter an exercise designed to connect you to your future self before moving into an exploration of the many different aspects of your inner world.

❀ Present-Day-Self Questionnaire

Instructions: Write down your answers to these questions here or in your journal or notebook. If you get stuck or feel like you don't know the answer to the question, you can leave it blank or write "I'm not sure" in the space.

1. The three words I'd use to describe myself are _____, _____, and _____.

2. The three words my closest friend would use to describe me are _____, _____, and _____.

3. My greatest strength or asset is _____.

4. Something I could talk about for hours is _____.

5. I've been told that other people admire me for _____.

6. The thing people ask me for help with most often is _____ _____.

7. I think the most important thing in life is _____.

8. If money weren't an issue, I'd want to do _____ every day.

9. The life areas I feel strong in are _____.

10. The life areas I struggle with are _____.

11. My favorite thing about my life is _____.

12. My least favorite thing about my life is _____.

13. My favorite sweet snack is _____.

14. My favorite salty snack is _____.

15. My favorite meal is _____.

16. My favorite time of day is _____.

17. My favorite type of music is _____.

18. My favorite types of movies are _____.

19. Something I think I should like but really don't is _____.

20. Something I think I shouldn't like but really do is _____.

21. Something I'm really hard on myself about is _____.

22. I would really like people to understand that I _____.

23. It would be nice if someone could help me with _____.

24. Something I'm proud of myself for overcoming is _____.

25. My goal with this workbook is to _____.

Check-In

Instructions: Either think about the following questions or write about them in your journal.

- How was doing the Present-Day-Self Questionnaire for you?
- Did you find it easy or hard to fill in the blanks?
- Do a quick scan of your body to see how it feels after doing this exercise. Do you feel numb, dissociated, or floaty? Edgy, anxious, or irritable? Consider taking a minute to stretch, get a drink of water, or pause before moving on to the next questions.
- How are you doing with your daily practice?

Observation: One takeaway from this work is:

_____

Recommendation: Something I can do with this information is:

_____

💭 Past-Self Questionnaire

Instructions: Write down your answers to these questions here or in your journal or notebook. If you get stuck or feel like you don't know the answer to the question, you can leave it blank or write "I'm not sure" in the space. Trigger warning: These questions sometimes can elicit uncomfortable feelings or body sensations. If you start to feel unsafe or in distress, do not force yourself to continue.

1. When I was a child, I wanted to _____ when I grew up.

2. My favorite book, movie, TV show, or story as a kid was _____.

3. The best quality about my mother was _____.
   (If you didn't have a mother, you can use any female caregiver. If you didn't have a female caregiver, you can leave this blank.)

4. The worst quality about my mother was _____.
   (If you didn't have a mother, you can use any female caregiver. If you didn't have a female caregiver, you can leave this blank.)

5. The best quality about my father was _____.
   (If you didn't have a father, you can use any male caregiver. If you didn't have a male caregiver, you can leave this blank.)

6. The worst quality about my father was _____.
   (If you didn't have a father, you can use any male caregiver. If you didn't have a male caregiver, you can leave this blank.)

7. As a child, what I learned about being an adult was _____.

8. As a child, what I learned about money was _____.

9. As a child, what I learned about food was _____.

10. As a child, what I learned about making mistakes was _____.

11. As a child, I learned I needed to _____ to get approval.

12. As a child, I loved _____.

13. As a child, I hated _____.

14. My favorite childhood friend was _____.
    (If you didn't have childhood friends, you can use an imaginary friend or an animal or leave this blank.)

15. What I really liked about my favorite childhood friend was _____
    _____.

16. My favorite childhood treat was _____.

17. My favorite childhood memory is _____.

18. The one word I'd use to describe myself as a child is _____.

19. One thing I really wanted as a child but never got to do or have was _____
    _____.

20. My favorite childhood toy was _____.

21. What was the relationship between your parents when you were born? _____
    _____.

22. Did you have a favorite adult in childhood? If so, who? _____
    _____.

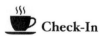 **Check-In**

Instructions: Either think about the following questions or write about them in your journal.

▸ How was doing the Past-Self Questionnaire for you?

▸ Did you find it easy or hard to fill in the blanks?

▸ Do a quick scan of your body to see how it feels after doing this exercise. Do you feel numb, dissociated, or floaty? Edgy, anxious, or irritable? Consider taking a minute to stretch, get a drink of water, or pause before moving on to the next questions.

▸ How are you doing with your daily practice?

Observation: One takeaway from this work is:

_____

Recommendation: Something I can do with this information is:

_____

 Wisdom from Your Future Self

Instructions: Think about the best version of yourself two days, two weeks, two months, and two years from now. Pretend that your life is headed in the direction of your dreams and that you are fully on track to do, be, or have everything you want. Either think about or write a letter to your current self from your future self in the following spaces or in your notebook. What wisdom and encouragement does future you want to share?

My future self two days from now wants me to know:

My future self two weeks from now wants me to know:

My future self two months from now wants me to know:

My future self two years from now wants me to know:

At this point, let's take a break from feelings and memories and mind stuff and shift to a quick inventory of the physical body you call home.

Parts Work

Have you ever felt like part of you knew *exactly* what you were supposed to do, nevertheless you ended up doing the complete opposite? Ever felt like you were stuck in a tug-of-war with yourself, trying to force yourself to do something when everything in you was screaming to do something else?

Welcome to the world of parts.

In his book *Internal Family Systems Therapy*, Dr. Richard Schwartz puts it like this: "A part is not just a temporary emotional state or habitual thought pattern. Instead, it is a discrete and autonomous mental system that has an idiosyncratic range of emotion, style of expression, set of abilities, desires, and view of the world. In other words, it is as if we each contain a society of people, each of whom is at a different age and has different interests, talents, and temperaments."

⚡ *Self*-awareness requires *parts*-awareness.

Some people get nervous when they hear about the different "parts" of the personality and often ask, "Does this mean I have multiple personality disorder?"*

No.

What is formerly known as multiple personality disorder (MPD) is now referred to as dissociative identity disorder (DID). Having different "parts" of your personality is *not* the same as having dissociative identity disorder.

If you've seen Pixar's movie *Inside Out*, the idea of inner parts will sound familiar. If you haven't seen it (ten out of ten recommend you do), *Inside Out* is about the colorful cast of characters inside the protagonist Riley's mind. The story emphasizes why all feelings—even sadness and anger—are important and useful. In the movie, one of the inner parts (Joy) says, "Do you ever look at someone and wonder, 'What is going on inside their head?' Well, I know. I know Riley's head." The next set of exercises helps you know what's going on inside your own head.

---

*Dissociative identity disorder is a reasonable response to extreme trauma and is often misunderstood and stigmatized.

💭 Parts Inventory Checklist

Instructions: Read the statements in the following chart, and put a check mark next to any that resonate with you.

	Even though sometimes I know there's no reason to be worried, there's this other part of me that always feels worried.
	Even when I'm reassured that everything is okay, it feels like there's another part of me that doesn't really believe it.
	I know logically that I'm not a fraud, but there's this other part of me that constantly has imposter syndrome.
	Sometimes I'm on my phone scrolling and I know I should put it down, but there's another part of me that can't seem to stop watching video after video.
	When I get angry, sometimes it feels like this other part of me takes over and I end up saying and doing things I later wish I hadn't.
	When I feel anxious, I sometimes feel silly because even though I know logically everything is safe, there's another part of me that won't calm down no matter what I say or do.
	Even though I know a certain relationship is unhealthy, there's part of me that really doesn't want to give it up and is afraid to lose the person.
	Logically I know I'm a grown person, but sometimes it really doesn't feel like it.

Even though we all have different life experiences, backgrounds, and genetic makeups, most people end up checking all the boxes. Why? Because all of us are made of different parts. Or as Walt Whitman famously wrote, "I am large. I contain multitudes."

What does that mean? Consider the world around you:

- ▸ A tree is one organism, but it is made of multiple parts, including branches, bark, roots, and leaves, each with different needs. You don't solve a root problem with a leaf solution.
- ▸ A car is one object, but it is made of multiple parts, including wheels, seats, a gas tank, and an engine, each with different functions. You don't expect the windshield wipers to do the job of the engine.

▸ Earth is one planet made of multiple parts, including landmasses, bodies of water, and weather systems, each separate and autonomous but still part of the whole.

⌗━O Every complex system is made of multiple parts, including your personality.

You probably have no trouble thinking of your physical body as a whole thing containing multiple parts like internal organs, systems, and cells. Yet many of us were taught that our "personality" is a whole thing, end of story.

This is inaccurate.

Your personality, like any system, is made of multiple parts, and each part has different needs and responds to different triggers and stimuli, just like the body, trees, cars, and planets. Viewing the personality in terms of parts is called the "multiplicity of mind" framework, and it's been around for thousands of years.* Healing modalities that operate within this framework include Inner Child, Gestalt, Voice Dialogue, and my personal favorite, a therapeutic approach called Internal Family Systems (IFS). The goal of IFS is to understand and connect with all parts of ourselves through the lens of curiosity and compassion. The Self is like the orchestra conductor, head coach, or CEO of your internal system. The goal of healing isn't to get rid of your parts. The goal of healing is to develop a relationship with your parts.

⌗━O The Self's job is to conduct the inner orchestra, coach the team, or run the company with skill, kindness, and firmness.

When you understand that *all* parts of yourself have value—even the ones you don't like— you can break long-standing patterns of negative thinking, procrastination, and self-

---

*Parts can be found in ancient Greece and also in the Bible—Christianity thinks of God as three distinct parts (Father, Son, and Holy Spirit), and one of the apostles complained that although he knew what he was supposed to do, a part of him kept doing the opposite.

sabotage. Getting to know all the parts of your inner world is necessary to feel embodied, whole, and in the driver's seat of your life. It's helpful to take an inventory of all the parts of yourself, without judgment or shame. A skillful conductor knows the strengths of their musicians,* a competent coach knows how to bring forth the best in their players, and top leaders understand the people they are tasked to serve.

 Parts Inventory

Instructions: Fill in the blanks.

There's a part of me that gets scared when _____.

When this part gets scared, I often choose to _____.

There's a part of me that gets angry when _____.

When this part gets angry, I often end up _____.

There's a part of me that often chooses to _____

    when I'd rather be doing _____.

When I get really overwhelmed, it feels like parts of me take over and _____

_____.

Parts of me feel depressed when _____.

When these parts feel depressed, I usually _____.

Parts of me feel anxious when _____.

When these parts get anxious, I sometimes _____.

Parts of me really want to _____.

Parts of me are afraid if I do what I want to do, then _____

_____ will happen.

---

*Conductors are not just there for show. To see what is really happening on that podium, check out this video: https://www.youtube.com/watch?v=diwV2HGKerE or search for "What does a conductor do?"

Parts of me are afraid if I get what I want, then _____

_____ will happen.*

🪷 All Parts Are Welcome†

Instructions: In IFS, our credo is "All parts are welcome!" Here is an exercise to help you welcome all of your parts.

1. Turn your attention inside and begin with this offer: *I want to help anyone who needs help. To do that, I need to know all of you.*
2. Then provide this information: *If you overwhelm me, I can't be there to help you.*
3. And make this request: *Please be here with me rather than taking me over, and, when you're ready, let me know who are you are. I will write this down.*
4. Write down the parts (thoughts, feelings, or sensations) that you hear, see, or sense inside yourself. Use extra paper if needed.

_____

_____

_____

_____

_____

Your Inner Critic

What would change if you thought of your inner critic as a scared child instead of as an angry parent or enraged boss?

---

* Maria Bamford made a valid point when she said, "My therapist says I'm afraid of success. I guess I could understand that because after all, fulfilling my potential would REALLY cut into my sitting-around time."

† This exercise was created by Frank Anderson, MD, psychiatrist, and one of the top minds in the IFS world, and is from Anderson, Sweezy, and Schwartz, *Internal Family Systems Skills Training Manual*. Used with permission.

Most of us were taught to fear and despise the voice inside us who tells us we aren't good enough, smart enough, lovable enough, or worthy enough. You likely learned that you needed to banish, destroy, or silence the voice of your inner critic. But when you fight with your parts, you release a cascade of stress hormones and uncomfortable body sensations, including anxiety and stress.

Your inner critic is not a demon to be slain or a nuisance to be banished; it is a valuable part of your inner society stuck in a crappy job—protecting you from pain.* In *No Bad Parts*, Dr. Richard Schwartz writes: "Your protectors' goals for your life revolve around keeping you away from all that pain, shame, loneliness, and fear, and they use a wide array of tools to meet those goals—achievements, substances, food, entertainment, shopping, sex, obsession with your appearance, caretaking, meditation, money, and so on."

When it comes to your inner critic, you may have tried to ignore, distract yourself from, or numb away its messages. You may have tried fighting with your inner critic. You may have tried talking yourself out of what your inner critic said, or you may have believed its words to be true.

None of these approaches usually work.

Instead of thinking of your inner critic as a mean bully, egoic overlord, or relentless boss, what if you thought of it as a terrified toddler? It feels very different when a three-year-old says, "I hate you!" than when someone you respect says you're not worthy. It feels very different when a frightened child says, "Go away!" than when someone you admire says, "You're not acceptable."

Ignoring a toddler, fighting with a toddler, or believing what a toddler says seems silly and pointless, because what a scared child needs is a competent and curious adult to tend to their fear (and to ensure they don't hurt themselves or anyone else). Sometimes our efforts to silence the inner critic fails because we mistake it for a *parent* instead of a *part*. When a toddler melts down, you're not going to talk them out of their feelings. Nor are you going to be able to simply walk away and expect a good outcome. Instead, a competent and caring caregiver knows how to sit with and respond to a toddler's big feelings rather than reacting with anger or fear. (Easier said than done.)

---

*Disclaimer: The intention of your protector parts is to help you, but that doesn't mean all the actions of your protector parts are "good" or acceptable. Explanation is not a synonym for excuse.

Rather than trying to eliminate your inner critic, what would happen if you tried to *understand* them? Understanding the inner critic *doesn't* mean you agree with or listen to their messages. Understanding the inner critic means you can listen for the fear beneath the words and respond as a caring parent, competent leader, or confident head coach.

It can help to think of the inner critic as a *child*-aged part instead of as a parent-aged part.

Your Inner Critic

Instructions: Consider the stressors in your life and the ways your inner critic might be upset, worried, or trying to help you. Maybe it's trying to help prevent you from failing. Maybe it's trying to help avoid embarrassment or looking weak. Maybe it thinks if you stay silent and small, you'll stay safe. Journal your own thoughts, or use the following prompts to get started.

› If my inner critic was a toddler throwing a tantrum, what would be different about the significance I attach to their words?

- If my inner critic was a scared child, how would I respond to their fears?
- If my inner critic was an adolescent trying to prevent me from getting bullied, how would I feel toward them?
- If my inner critic was a teenager about to start a new school, how would I support them?

The Secret to Self-Talk

Most of us would never talk to our friends the way we talk to ourselves. Self-talk can often be critical, shaming, and flat-out mean.

Inner Monologue Zingers

Instructions: Circle any of the following statements you've ever thought or said.

Why did I say that?
Why didn't I say that?
Why did I do that?
Why didn't I do that?
What was I thinking?
How could I have been so stupid?
I messed up again.
I can't do it.
I can't stop doing it.
I'm so unattractive.
I hate my body.
I'll never get it right.
I should be doing more.
I'm a bad friend.

I'm not lovable.

If they really knew me, they wouldn't like me.

Scoring: If you circled any of these statements, you may benefit from the next set of exercises.

Inner Monologue Versus Inner Dialogue

When you use the words *I* and *me* to talk to yourself, it's easy to forget that you are just as worthy of care and respect as the people around you. The trick to effective self-talk is to turn your inner *monologue* into an inner *dialogue*.

What does that mean?

When you speak to yourself using your name, your pronouns, or the word *you* (as if you were speaking to someone else), you create space for yourself to exist. Viktor Frankl wrote, "Between stimulus and response there is a space. In that space is our power to choose our response. In our response lies our growth and our freedom." Third-person self-talk creates space for compassion and capacity for *responding* to stressors rather than *reacting* to triggers. If I were using third-person self-talk, it would sound something like this:

- ▸ "Britt, I noticed you just said . . ."
- ▸ "There's a part of me right now that wants to hide. She's worried about . . ."
- ▸ "Hi, Britt. I know you're super stressed right now. That makes sense."
- ▸ "Wow. There are parts of me right now that feel very overwhelmed."

It feels uncomfortably odd when you first start speaking to yourself this way. Many of my clients initially scoff and say, "This is ridiculous. I feel ridiculous doing this. *No one* talks this way." And they're right. This way of speaking to yourself and thinking about yourself *is* ridiculous—it's a completely abnormal way to speak and think. But if the "normal" way was useful, you likely wouldn't be reading this book.

⚲ **Just because something is normal does not mean it is healthy.**

One of the most powerful tools used by therapists is called the "empty-chair technique." On the American Psychological Association's *APA Dictionary of Psychology* website, the empty-chair technique is defined as "a technique originating in gestalt therapy* in which the client conducts an emotional dialogue with some aspect of themself or some significant person (e.g., a parent) who is imagined to be sitting in an empty chair during the session."† The next exercise is based on this technique.

👣 **Empty-Chair-Inspired Exercise**

Instructions: Follow the steps below.

Step 1: Choose an object to represent a part of yourself that feels scared, anxious, frustrated, or sad. I've found this exercise works best when the object you choose has significance for you, like a favorite toy from childhood or a treasured item you got on Etsy or at a local thrift store, but it also can be a coffee cup, an empty box, or a bottle of hand sanitizer—it doesn't matter. It matters more that you try the exercise than it does which object you select.

Step 2: Place the object on a chair across from you or on the couch next to you. Then, reassure, encourage, or say whatever supportive things to the object you'd say to a friend. Yes, you will feel bonkers doing this. Yes, do it anyway.

> *Note: You can use the same object to represent all your parts, or you can select several objects to represent different age groups—one object for young child parts, one for adolescent or teen parts, one for adult parts, etc.*

---

*Gestalt therapy is "a phenomenological-existential therapy founded by Frederick (Fritz) and Laura Perls in the 1940s. It teaches therapists and patients the phenomenological method of awareness, in which perceiving, feeling, and acting are distinguished from interpreting and reshuffling preexisting attitudes." From Gary Yontef, PhD, "Gestalt Therapy: An Introduction," The Gestalt Therapy Network, https://www.gestalt.org/yontef.htm.

† "Empty-chair technique," *APA Dictionary of Psychology*, American Psychological Association, https://dictionary .apa.org/empty-chair-technique.

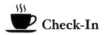 **Check-In**

Instructions: Either think about the following questions or write about them in your journal.

- What was the hardest part of the parts-work exercises? What was the easiest?
- Did you try the All Parts Are Welcome exercise? If not, consider going back and trying it. If you did, which part was the hardest for you to welcome? What job might this part be doing to try to help protect you?
- How are you doing with your daily practice?

Observation: One takeaway from this work is:

_____

Recommendation: Something I can do with this information is:

_____

The Eight C's of Self-Leadership

The Eight C's of Self-Leadership is what the Internal Family Systems model uses to describe the qualities of the Self, which is the inner leader. Here are the eight C's:

1. Calmness*
2. Clarity
3. Curiosity

---

*"Calmness" in the IFS model does not necessarily mean "serene" or "blissful." Self can be calm *and* angry, calm *and* passionate, etc. The word *calm* refers to the ability to maintain a sense of choice and control of emotional expression rather than being driven by emotions.

4. Compassion
5. Confidence
6. Courage
7. Creativity
8. Connectedness

 Self-Leadership Inventory

Instructions: Consider the qualities of Self-leadership listed in the following chart. On a scale of one to ten (with one being the least often and ten, the most often), rank how often you feel like you embody each quality. Then, fill in the boxes with situations when you feel the least like the quality and when you feel the most like the quality.

Quality	Rank (One to Ten)	When Do I Feel the Least Like This?	When Do I Feel the Most Like This?
Calmness			
Clarity			
Curiosity			
Compassion			
Confidence			

Quality	Rank (One to Ten)	When Do I Feel the Least Like This?	When Do I Feel the Most Like This?
Courage			
Creativity			
Connectedness			

Rather than speaking to yourself with the biting, critical, harsh voice of a bully, Self-Leadership allows you to approach your parts with the persuasive skill and genuine heart of a great leader or coach. Because most of us were not taught to approach our inner selves this way, it can be helpful to look to the movies for examples of what to do before trying it yourself.

Movie Inspiration

Instructions: For this exercise, you'll watch movie or TV clips in which leaders successfully inspire their people. It is important to look at fictional characters who do *not* resort to guilt, shame, or rage.

BATTLEFIELD LEADERSHIP

Step 1: Watch a movie or TV clip in which an inspirational speech is given during a battle scene. You can search online for clips of your own, or I recommend Aragorn's "This day we fight!" speech from *The Lord of the Rings: The Return of the King*.

Step 2: Either use the space on the next page or write in your journal or notebook what stood out as you watched the clip. Notice the differences in the crowd—did it matter? Were they fighting among themselves? Notice the way the leader approached their people—what qualities did they embody?

_____

_____

_____

_____

LOCKER-ROOM LEADERSHIP

Step 1: Watch a movie or TV clip of a locker-room scene. You can search online for clips of your own, or I recommend the *Gridiron Gang* locker-room scene in which Dwayne "The Rock" Johnson gives one of the most heartfelt and motivational speeches ever. You also can look up the "We cannot lose" scene from *We Are Marshall*. Or just watch every single episode of *Ted Lasso*. In each scene, notice how the coach demonstrates empathy and humanity while still maintaining authority.

Step 2: Either use the space below or write in your journal or notebook what stood out as you watched the clip. Notice the differences in the crowd—did it matter? Were they fighting among themselves? Notice the way the leader approached their people—what qualities did they embody?

_____

_____

_____

_____

Your Turn: Parts Dialogue

Now that you've watched examples of leadership demonstrated by other people, it's time to apply those qualities to your inner dialogue. Warning: The next three exercises are among the silliest sounding of all the therapy tasks I've ever seen, heard, or done. I invite you to consider trying them anyway. I'll reiterate—just because something is normal does not mean it's healthy. And just because something is wildly uncomfortable doesn't mean it isn't incredibly effective.

Uncomfortable Task 1: Voicemail Pep Talk

Instructions: Leave yourself a voicemail (or a voice memo) giving yourself a pep talk for something you need to do. It can be a presentation at work, a hard conversation with your family, or something as simple as encouraging yourself to start doing that thing you've been avoiding. Then listen to it at least three times.

Disclaimer: Most people cringe at the sound of their own voice. There's even a term for it—*voice confrontation*. Voice confrontation happens for many reasons, one of which is that most people aren't used to hearing what their recorded voice sounds like. Giving yourself a voicemail pep talk allows you to self-dialogue while *also* getting used to the sound of your own voice. With enough time and practice, you'll register your own voice as a friendly ally, not a cringey enemy.

Uncomfortable Task 2: Evening and Morning Encouragement

Instructions: Follow the steps below.

Step 1: Leave yourself a voicemail to listen to in the morning. Say anything in this voicemail your parts need to hear. That can be encouraging them to get out of bed, reminding them that not everything is hopeless, reminding them of their resources (people, places, or things available to them), or saying anything else that would be helpful to hear in the morning.

Step 2: Repeat, recording a voicemail to listen to in the evening.

> *Note: This is not an exercise in toxic positivity. You do not need to be 100 percent positive or grateful. Sometimes, the best pep talk is one that can hold two truths at once, such as, "This is going to be a hard day. It is going to be a really hard day. But I'm here to get you through it."*

Step 3: Listen to the morning voicemail every morning and the evening voicemail every evening. The more you practice this, the less you will hate the sound of your voice and the more your parts will begin to feel seen and heard.

❧ Uncomfortable Task 3: Dominant/Nondominant Journaling

Instructions: Follow the steps below.

Step 1: You'll need two pens or markers and a notebook or journal for this exercise.

Step 2: Choose a part with which you want to dialogue. Be sure that you are feeling open and curious toward the part before trying this exercise. (Trying to practice this exercise with a part you don't like is not recommended.)

Step 3: Place your notebook in front of you where you can write in it. Hold one pen in your dominant hand (the hand you normally use), and hold another pen in your nondominant hand (the one you don't normally use).

Step 4: With your dominant hand, write down questions to ask this part. With your nondominant hand, write down the answers. You can make up questions of your own or use the following ten prompts.

> *Note: Remember to implement the leadership qualities you read earlier, and try to express compassion and curiosity toward the part. It may feel like your nondominant hand is writing without your awareness, or it may feel like you are just making things up. Both feelings are completely normal.*

1. Hi, part. I'm curious about you. Would you like to talk to me today?
2. How old are you?
3. What are your favorite things to do?
4. What are your favorite foods?
5. What are your favorite movies?

6. What is your favorite kind of music?
7. What would you like me to know about you?
8. What do you wish I would do for you?
9. How old do you think I am?
10. I can keep you safe by _____.

    [List at least three ways you can keep this part safe.] What do you think about that?

☕ Check-In

Instructions: Either think about the following questions or write about them in your journal.

▸ What was the hardest of the awkward tasks? What was the easiest?

▸ Did you try any of the awkward tasks? If not, consider going back and trying one or several. If listening to your own voice causes you too much distress, consider asking a friend to help you by leaving you the voicemails for the time being.

▸ How are you doing with your daily practice?

Observation: One takeaway from this work is:

_____

Recommendation: Something I can do with this information is:

_____

Self-Care Versus Parts-Care

Sometimes your best efforts at self-care fall flat because the part of you that needs attention doesn't respond to the intervention you're trying to implement. For your self-care efforts to work, your coping skills need to developmentally match the part in need of help. Asking yourself how old you feel when triggered can help you decide on the best action to take to de-escalate your system. For example:

- If you feel like a frightened toddler when triggered, a "toddler parts-care" intervention might be a weighted blanket, hug, or reassurance.
- If you feel like an angry teenager when triggered, a "teenage parts-care" intervention might be listening to loud music, crunching on Flamin' Hot Cheetos, or yelling in your car.
- If you feel like a lonely adolescent when triggered, an "adolescent parts-care" intervention might be spending time with friends.

■━O Effective *self*-care requires *parts* awareness.

When you implement adult coping skills for developmentally younger parts, the mismatch likely will result in you feeling like there is something wrong with *you*. There isn't. The next exercise gives you a menu of parts-care activities you can have at your disposal when you need them. Trying to figure out what you need while you are triggered can be tricky at best and next to impossible at worst. Having a list handy can help keep your brain from spinning into an emotional regression, which is what happens when you feel smaller and younger than your chronological age.

💭 Parts-Care Inventory

Instructions: Follow the steps below.

Step 1: Each of the circles in the following graphic contains a developmental age. In the box below each circle, write a list of coping strategies that would be a good fit for that age. This is your parts-care inventory.

Step 2: When you're triggered, ask yourself, "How old do I feel right now?"

Step 3: Whatever age you answered in step 2, choose a coping strategy from that box.

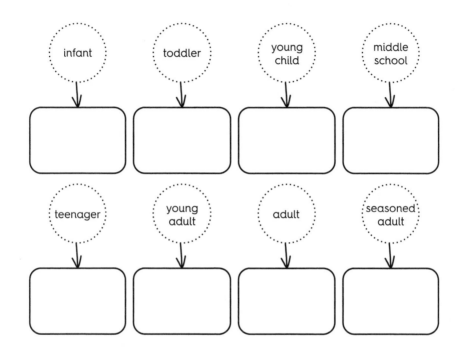

Some people are concerned that all this self-exploration and parts-care work will create a narcissistic monster. "I don't want to become full of myself" is a concern I hear when people begin to shift from people-pleasing to parts-pleasing. My response?

It's important to be full of your Self. People with a full tank of Self energy do not act selfish, mean, or horrible.

When we say someone is "so full of themselves," what we really mean is "they have zero access to their Self." People who are full of Self embody the best qualities humanity has to offer—compassion, curiosity, creativity, and love. Moreover:

- ▸ Full people know who they are and allow themselves to take up space.
- ▸ Full people don't take things personally and can detach their Self worth from other people's actions.
- ▸ Full people don't put on airs in efforts to justify their existence.
- ▸ Full people aren't arrogant; arrogance isn't necessary if you know your Self.

Without access to Self, we stay fully dependent on external people and things for our internal well-being. It's good to be "full of Self." The world could use a lot more people who are full of Self.

⌗O Bottom-Line Takeaways

- ▸ Knowing who you are requires a brave exploration of your inner world.
- ▸ Ignoring yourself almost never goes well.
- ▸ It can be scary to go inside your mind and evaluate your thoughts.
- ▸ It's good to have full access to Self.
- ▸ All complex systems are made of parts, including your personality.
- ▸ Self-care requires parts-care.
- ▸ Self-awareness requires parts-awareness.
- ▸ All parts of your inner world have value.
- ▸ Reframing your inner critic as a scared and angry toddler can help make it seem less scary.
- ▸ The secret of self-talk is to turn your inner monologue into an inner dialogue.

DOS AND DON'TS OF MAKING FRIENDS WITH YOUR MIND

Do	Don't
Remind yourself that if your body can be one thing made of parts, so can your personality.	Assume that your personality is a single thing that is either "healthy" or "disordered."
Recognize that doing this work can be difficult.	Ignore the reality that *not* doing this work is also difficult.
Extend compassion to yourself for having parts who want to say or do bad things.	Give yourself a pass for bad behavior. All parts are welcome; all behavior is not.
Ask yourself how old you feel when you're triggered.	Expect an adult coping skill to work for a younger part.

End-of-Level Challenge

In your journal, respond to these prompts:

- ▸ Growing up, what did I learn about self-care and nurture?
- ▸ Where did these ideas come from?
- ▸ Do I want to continue to believe these things?
- ▸ What would I change?

Congratulations! You've reached the end of this part. Use the space below for final observations and recommendations:

Observations:

_____

_____

_____

Recommendations:

_____

_____

_____

PART 3

Humaning Is Messy

How to Create Skillful Relationships

This part covers dating and intimacy. If you're not in (or looking for) a romantic relationship, there's also plenty of information here on boundaries and codependency that applies to friendships, family, and work relationships.

I'm not strange, weird, off, nor crazy, my reality is just different from yours.

—Lewis Carroll, *Alice in Wonderland*

Back in the pre-Google era, I didn't have access to a dating guide, but you'll get to create one here so you can avoid the more extreme shenanigans of the dating world I experienced. If you're already coupled, throupled, or in any other type of relationship, you can skip ahead to the intimacy tasks. We'll also look at how to handle codependency, how to set boundaries, and what to do with difficult family dynamics.

Dating

Have you ever been given really, *really* bad advice about your relationships? Ludicrous dating suggestions are nothing new. Some vintage gems include these:

- ▸ "Stand in a corner and cry softly. Chances are good he'll come over and find out what's wrong." (*McCall's* magazine article, 1958)

- ▸ "Do not allow yourself in the habit of joking with your companions. This tends to cultivate severe sarcasm, which is a bad habit of the tongue." (*How to Be a Lady*, 1850)

- ▸ "Don't talk too much and, above all, don't talk about yourself, ever." (*How to Win and Hold a Husband*, 1939)

Nineteenth- and early twentieth-century dating wisdom is clearly antiquated, but you don't have to time-warp very far back to find cringeworthy recommendations:

- "Looking at someone first is a dead giveaway of interest . . . Instead, look down at the table or your food, or simply survey the crowd at the restaurant." (*The Rules*, 1995)

- "At a casual restaurant, lose the fork in favor of your fingers. Look him in the eye while you lick off any excess salt or sauce." (Women's magazine, early 2000s)

- "At the end of the night, tease him with a juicy nugget of info. ('Next time, remind me to tell you about my crazy spring break in Daytona.') He'll push you to spill, but wave him off and say, 'Sorry—got to get inside! It's the kind of story that needs telling over cheese fries . . .'" (*Seventeen Ultimate Guide to Guys*, 2013)

Journal Prompt: Best and Worst Advice

Instructions: Consider the dating advice you've received from well-meaning friends and family members. Either use the space below or write in your journal the best and worst advice you've received. Think about or journal about how reading this advice makes you feel. Would you give this advice to someone?

_____

_____

_____

_____

_____

It is impossible to cover every conceivable aspect of relationships in a single book—anyone who claims otherwise is likely to be selling something. This material is intended to give you just the basics of dating neuroscience so you can start training your brain to do what you *want* it to do rather than what it's *wired* to do.

⌐O The human brain is *not* wired for modern dating.

The Neuroscience of Dating

As author Abhijit Naskar put it in *The Art of Neuroscience in Everything*, "A fulfilling long-term relationship is not accomplished by just finding 'the one.' It is rather a cooperation between two passionate and highly motivated partners working together, figuring out every single situation holding hands." The challenge? To create cooperation between partners, you need logic and reason.

Think of logic and reason as your brain's parents. When you start dating someone new, your parents go out of town and the rest of your brain throws a chemical cocktail party where things get *really* rowdy.*

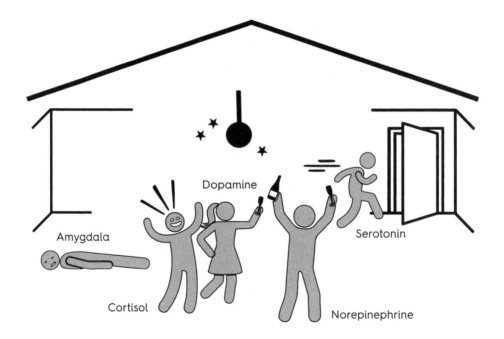

*For a funny and easy-to-remember overview of dating neuroscience, check out NPR's "A Neuroscience Love Song" at https://www.npr.org/sections/health-shots/2018/02/13/584645628/your-besotted-brain-a-neuroscience-love-song.

The Neuroscience Cocktail Party[*]

- **Cortisol:** Cortisol is a stress hormone. Dating causes cortisol to surge through your body, creating a crisis state. This causes you to feel edgy and anxious.

- **Dopamine:** Dopamine is a stimulant involved with the reward circuit of your brain. This compels you to seek pleasure and repeat behaviors—even if the behaviors are not good for you.

- **Norepinephrine:** Norepinephrine (also called noradrenaline) is a hormone and chemical messenger that makes you feel giddy, alert, and unable to eat or sleep.

- **Serotonin:** Serotonin has many functions, one of which is to help prevent obsessive thinking. Serotonin leaves the party when you start dating someone new. The drop in serotonin causes you to feel obsessive and panicky. This is why you check your phone a thousand times a day and can't stop your mind from zooming around in circles.

- **Amygdala:** Your amygdala is the alarm system of your brain. During dating, the amygdala gets deactivated so your brain is less likely to tell you, "No. Stop. Don't date that person. We've already done this. Twice."

⊶ Dating someone new causes your brain to go into spring break mode.

You would never take a tequila shot or chomp down a few gummies and then expect to make solid decisions about your business or finances. Yet we do this all the time with dating and then feel confused when things don't work out. No shame if you've experienced this—we were all taught to chase the fairy tale (even though most fairy tales end in gruesome and non-family-friendly ways).

---

[*] This information is based on the most current neuroscience in 2022. Science is always subject to change without notice.

The following exercises give you a custom-tailored dating plan. When your brain gets soggy, it's hard to take care of basic needs like food and sleep, let alone higher-level functions like conscious relationship design. The first three exercises focus on partner selection (traffic light, dating rulebook, trigger compatibility). The next three cover self-awareness (SWOT analysis, dating profile pics, rom-com detox), and the final three are science-based strategies to support your brain through a breakup (ex-file, movie relationship quiz, withdrawal plan).

Picking Your Partner(s): How to Organize the Selection Process

Using a traffic light as a visual reference, this first exercise helps you identify, organize, and then recognize in the heat of battle those qualities you want in a partner:

- ▸ Green light qualities are always acceptable.
- ▸ Yellow light qualities are not deal-breakers but are things that can trend toward problematic (and a sign you should go *very* slowly).
- ▸ Red light qualities immediately disqualify someone from consideration.

Creating a traffic light dating system helps *dramatically* cut down on wasted time because you'll be clear on your nonnegotiables from the start. Putting this plan in writing means you're less likely to justify red light qualities with thoughts like, *Well yeah, he's married, but his divorce is* almost *finalized* or *I know she is actively struggling with substance abuse, but she's so* amazing and has a *really* good plan for getting sober. If you discover a red light quality, the answer to the "Should I date them?" question is always no or not yet.

🔑 You can be in a relationship only with a person, *not* with their potential.

💬 Partner Selection 1: Red Light, Green Light, One, Two, Three

Instructions: Write down your green, yellow, and red light qualities in the spaces below. I've added a few to get you started. If you're comfortable doing so, review and revise these qualities based on feedback from those who know and love you. Refer to this dating decision framework whenever you match with someone online or meet them in real life.

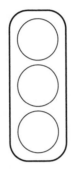

GREEN LIGHT QUALITIES (THINGS THAT ARE ALWAYS GOING TO BE ACCEPTABLE)

Doesn't lose their temper
Is kind to other people and animals

_____

_____

_____

_____

YELLOW LIGHT QUALITIES (THINGS THAT AREN'T NECESSARILY DEAL-BREAKERS BUT ARE IMPORTANT TO KEEP AN EYE ON AND A SIGN THAT MOVING VERY SLOWLY IS NECESSARY)

Oversharer
Just got out of a long relationship

_____

_____

_____

_____

RED LIGHT QUALITIES (THINGS THAT ARE AUTOMATIC, NONNEGOTIABLE DEAL-BREAKERS)

Married
Currently struggling with an addiction

_____

_____

_____

_____

As you read earlier, dating guidelines change dramatically with time. Advice that was sound even a few years ago quickly can become outdated at best and potentially harmful at worst. It's important to consider what rules make sense for *your* life. Following dating rules is easier said than done, so this exercise also prompts you to consider why your rules matter—and how to help yourself stick to them. Pro tip: share your list with a friend to help you keep yourself accountable.

💭 Partner Selection 2: Your Dating Rulebook

Instructions: Fill in the following chart. Everyone will have a different set of rules, but I've added a few universal ones to get you started. Many people resist the first rule, but remember, your brain is not equipped to skillfully handle hours-long dates early in a relationship. You wouldn't expect your body to run a marathon without training, and similarly, your brain needs time and practice before it can safely do the same.

✓ Dating Rule	! Why It's Important	♡ When It Will Be Difficult	? What I Can Do
No more than two hours for a first date.	Even though marathon dates feel good, too much togetherness causes my brain to confuse *intensity* with *intimacy*. Just because a thing feels good doesn't mean it's a good thing.	When we're really into each other and the conversation is flowing and feels easy and magical.	Plan something with my friends the same evening as the date so I have an excuse to leave.
No more than two drinks on a date.	It's hard to assess a potential partnership or make good decisions if I'm drunk.	When I'm nervous.	Plan a date where we can be doing something instead of staring at each other. Drink club soda and lime. Have a friend on standby I can text.
No trauma dumping (telling my most vulnerable stories on a first or second date).	Deep sharing is safest when there is trust, and trust requires consistent behavior over time.	When I feel a strong connection and feel compelled to immediately share my secrets (or ask about theirs).	Remind myself that people need to *earn* the right to my stories, and that only comes with time. The reverse is also true. If they're spilling their life story on a first date, that's a yellow light quality. (See the traffic light exercise.)

✓ Dating Rule	❗ Why It's Important	🦌 When It Will Be Difficult	❓ What I Can Do

Articles and blog posts about compatibility often focus on things like physical attraction, lifestyle, shared interests, and political affiliation, but trigger compatibility is rarely (if ever) mentioned. Trigger compatibility means that things that set off *your* inner alarm aren't in conflict with your partner's personality. For example, if you don't like loud noises, dating a drummer is probably not going to work. If receiving notifications all day reminds you of your controlling ex, you probably don't want to date someone who loves to constantly text, DM, snap, etc.

🗝 **Trigger compatibility often trumps personality compatibility.**

💭 **Partner Selection 3: Trigger Compatibility**

Instructions: Fill out the following chart. You don't need to automatically disqualify the types of people you list in the second column, but relationships with people who are likely to set off your triggers need to be pursued with extreme caution. Disclaimer: Trigger compatibility refers to *neutral* triggers, *not* to abuse.

My Triggers	Types of People Who Might Be Difficult to Date

☕ Check-In

Instructions: Either think about the following questions or write about them in your journal.

- Which of the partner selection exercises was easiest for you? Which was hardest?
- If you struggled to think of dating rules, google "rules for dating" and see if any resonate with you. If so, go back to the chart and add them.
- What surprised you about this work?
- How are you doing with your daily tasks?

Dating Self-Awareness: It's Not Always About Them

It can be easier (and a lot more fun) to focus outward on others than to focus inward on ourselves. But to minimize dating drama, it's important to do both. The next three exercises are designed to help you become mindful of your patterns, habits, and thoughts. The business world already has many tools and techniques that translate beautifully to this work. The one you'll use here is called a SWOT analysis (Strengths, Weaknesses, Opportunities, Threats).

Self-Awareness 1: Dating SWOT Analysis

Instructions: Using the bullet points as a guide, complete the chart on the next page. Keep in mind that strengths and weakness refer to you (internal) and opportunities and threats refer to your environment (external).

- **Strengths (internal):** What makes you a good partner? What qualities, behaviors, skills, or accomplishments are you most proud of?

- **Weaknesses (internal):** What are your personal qualities that could be problematic in a relationship? Do you have any habits or patterns that need to be retrained?

- **Opportunities (external):** What are your *current* resources to help you find a partner? Do you know any people who could make an introduction? Could any upcoming events provide a good opportunity to meet like-minded people? Is there technology that might help you?

- **Threats (external):** What are the environmental factors that could make dating difficult? Is it the dead of winter? Are you unable to leave the house? Does your boss require you to be on call 24/7?

Strengths	Weaknesses
Opportunities	Threats

One of the easiest ways to improve your position in the dating game is to assess your profile pictures. Thankfully, there are plenty of researchers who already devoted time and energy to figuring out what works so you don't have to. Consider the photos you're using in your dating profile to complete the exercise below. Disclaimer: This information refers to assessing potential romantic partners, not potential sex partners. If you want to have a fun, no-strings evening with that hot, shirtless, selfie-in-the-bathroom-taking Tinder match, be safe and have at it.

👣 Self-Awareness 2: Dating Profile Picture Inventory

Instructions: Consider the photos you have on your dating profile. Do they show you doing things you love? Are they reflective of your actual personality and likes and dislikes? Show your dating profile pictures to at least one (preferably three) people who know you well. Ask them for honest feedback about the photos and then make whatever adjustments you choose.

 **Self-Awareness 3: Love Song and Rom-Com Detox**

Instructions: For the next week, do not listen to music or watch movies or TV shows that glamorize, idealize, or focus in *any* way on love, relationships, or intimacy. Temporarily mute or unfollow any social media accounts with happy-looking couples living a perfect-looking life. If you can make it a week, consider extending this exercise to two weeks or even a month.

☕ Check-In

Instructions: Either think about the following questions or write about them in your journal.

- ▸ Are you willing to do the love song and rom-com detox?
- ▸ If so, what are your choices to help yourself stick to it?
- ▸ If this feels too difficult, are you willing to try it for at least a day? Or an evening?
- ▸ What will you gain from trying these tasks, and what do you lose by *not* trying them?
- ▸ How are you doing with your daily practice?

Observation: One takeaway from this work is:

_____

Recommendation: Something I can do with this information is:

_____

Supporting Your Brain Through a Breakup

Even though your brain processes physical and emotional pain differently, there's plenty of overlap. According to psychiatrist and *New York Times* best-selling author Dr. Daniel Amen, "When we lose a lover through a breakup or divorce, our brain gets confused and disoriented. Since the person lives in the neuronal connections, we expect to see them, hear them, feel them, and touch them. When we can't hold them or talk to them as we usually do, the brain centers where they live become inflamed searching for them. . . . Basically, we're a neurochemical mess."* A bad breakup can feel the same to your brain and body as detoxing from hard drugs. But there's an upside—because breakups impact not only your heart but also your brain, you can use neuroscience-based tools to help yourself cope.

Our brains love to filter out all the negative aspects of relationships and zoom focus on the good times. In the sex and love addiction recovery community, there's a technique called fantasy contamination. Fantasy contamination is like putting rat poison in a gourmet meal—if there's even a tiny bit, the whole thing becomes inedible. Here's an example if you're curious about this technique.

👣 Fantasy Contamination Ex-ercise

Instructions: Make a folder on your phone or computer, and dump anything in there that reminds you why the breakup was necessary. Your ex file can include screenshots of torture texts from them, screenshots of conversations you've had with your friends about them, and reminders to yourself about why things didn't work. Look at it every day for the next ninety days. Your brain is wired to continue to filter out important details, including information about why the relationship was toxic. This exercise helps put rat poison in the relationship fantasy.

---

*"Why Breaking Up Is So Hard on Your Brain," Amen Clinics, July 7, 2020, https://www.amenclinics.com/blog/why-breaking-up-is-so-hard-on-your-brain.

Your Brain on Breakups

When you detox from alcohol or drugs, there is a phase when you may experience post-acute withdrawal symptoms (PAWS). Breakups follow roughly the same timeline, assuming you are currently in a safe enough place, have resources to meet your basic needs, and currently are not being abused. The symptoms of PAWS include these:

Post-Acute Withdrawal Symptoms

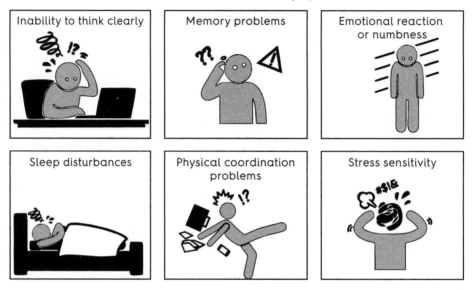

Sound familiar? If you are going through a rough breakup, you will experience nearly identical symptoms. It's important to know that your brain is reacting to the breakup as if it were in a chemical detox—because it is. The surge of stress hormones and reward chemicals is no longer active, so you literally are withdrawing from your own brain chemistry. If you don't know it's not just your heart but also your brain that reacts to breakups, you're likely to feel crazy. You aren't.

Coping with Breakup Withdrawal: Your Game Plan

Instructions: To best support your brain during the first two weeks of a breakup, you'll need a solid plan. Because hours eight through twenty-four create the most intensely felt pain, can you have a friend babysit your phone so you're not tempted to reach out to your ex? Can you take a mental health day from work? Can you throw yourself into a project as a distraction? Can you find people who might be willing to bring you food and check on you?

During acute withdrawal (day one), my plan is to:

_____

During peak withdrawal (days two and three), my plan is to:

_____

During post-acute withdrawal (days four through ten), my plan is to:

_____

Depression, numbness, and fatigue are likely to hit on days ten through fourteen. My plan for this time is to:

_____

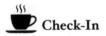 ## Check-In

Instructions: Either think about the following questions or write about them in your journal.

- ▸ What thoughts and feelings came up for you as you did the exercises?
- ▸ This work is difficult to do in isolation. Do you have any people with whom you can share your work and who can support and encourage you?
- ▸ How are you doing with your daily practice?

Intimate Relationships

Books, blogs, and social media posts about relationships should be required to include a giant warning label: "Couples work of any kind is *not* recommended if there is abuse."

Abuse is not a communication problem. Abuse is not a relationship problem. Abuse is an abuser problem—period. The National Domestic Violence Hotline says in no uncertain terms, "We're often asked how we feel about couples therapy, and whether we'd encourage that as a course of action. Our answer is loud and clear: **We at The Hotline do not encourage anyone in an abusive relationship to seek counseling with their partner.** Abuse is not a relationship problem. While there can be benefits for couples who undergo [couples] therapy, there's a great risk for any person who is being abused to attend therapy with their abusive partner. Relationship counseling can help partners understand each other, resolve difficult problems, and even help the couple gain a different perspective on their situation. It cannot, however, fix the unequal **power structure** that is characteristic of an abusive relationship."*

As a domestic violence survivor, I understand the difficulty of managing a dangerous situation (and the danger of trying to escape). If it were easy to walk away from abusive re-

---

*"Should I Go to Couples Therapy with My Abusive Partner?" National Domestic Violence Hotline, https://www .thehotline.org/resources/should-i-go-to-couples-therapy-with-my-abusive-partner.

lationships, everyone would do it. Before moving on to the exercises, use the following chart to assess your relationship.

Warning Signs of an Abusive Relationship

Instructions: Answer yes or no to the following prompts. If you answer Y to any of them, the relationship advice in this part does not apply. If you need help, the National Domestic Violence Hotline's website is thehotline.org, and the phone number is 1-800-799-SAFE (7233). Or you can text START to 88788.

Warning Sign	Y/N
You are afraid to make your partner angry.	
Your partner hits, slaps, or shoves you; blocks your path; or in any way uses physical intimidation when they're angry.	
Your partner is controlling, insists on knowing where you are and who you are friends with, and makes demands on your time.	
Your partner either withholds sex as a punishment or pressures you to have sex when you don't want to.	
Your partner accuses you of being crazy when you disagree with them or bring up an issue.	
You spend less time doing things you like because it upsets your partner.	
You feel like you're walking on eggshells around your partner.	
You constantly apologize for things you didn't do, say, or think.	
Your partner is the only one with access to your finances.	
Your partner yells, name-calls, or puts you down when they are angry.	
You are afraid to leave your partner.	
Your partner uses the silent treatment to punish you.	
You lie about your partner's behavior to your family and friends.	
You justify your partner's behavior because "they had a bad day" or because "they had a bad childhood."	
Your partner has threatened suicide if you leave.	

Relationship Tool Kit

The next exercises are divided into the following categories:

- ▸ Four relationship hacks to uplevel your relationship when things are going well
- ▸ Four O's: apologies versus amends
- ▸ Four techniques to prevent relationship ruptures
- ▸ Four relationship myths to bust

Four Relationship Hacks to Uplevel Your Relationship

When things are going well, try one—or all—of the following four tasks.

❧ 1. Uninterrupted Listening

Instructions: Using a timer, give each person ten minutes of completely uninterrupted time to talk about whatever they want. (Exception: Do not use this time to criticize the relationship. This is a task to try when things are going well, not an excuse to corner your partner.) During the ten minutes, the listening partner puts down their phone and actively listens (making eye contact, nodding, using body language to show interest). After the ten minutes are up, the listening partner summarizes what they heard. Then the listening partner either makes a validating statement ("Wow, that sounds really hard") or asks a question. Once complete, switch and repeat the steps. The formula for this task is as follows:

1. Listener listens for ten minutes; talker shares uninterrupted for ten minutes.
2. Listener summarizes.
3. Listener asks a clarifying question or says something validating.

👣 2. Explore Each Other's Worlds

You don't have to have the same interests and hobbies to be in a relationship. That said, expressing interest in each other's worlds is important to sustain intimacy.

Instructions: Choose from one of the two options below. Option one is good; option two is better. If your partner is willing, ask if they'd be open to switching and trying this with you.

1. Ask your partner to share with you about the current show they're watching, the music they're listening to, or the video game they're playing. If they play a sport, ask them to share about that. If they like talking business, take the deep dive.

2. Ask your partner if you can watch one of their shows, listen to their music, watch them play their video game, or engage in whatever their thing is. Your job is to actively engage with them and ask thoughtful questions or express interest even if their thing is not your thing. You can ask things like, "What do you love about this?" "What is your favorite thing about _____," or "Tell me more about how you got into _____."

❤️ 3. Love, Respect, Admire, Learn

When we get settled in relationships, it's easy to forget to consistently express appreciation and gratitude. This task can be done as often as you want (weekly, daily, or monthly) and can be done over text (good), written down in a note (better), or face-to-face (best).

Instructions: Either text the following, write it down in a note and leave it for your partner, or tell them when you're face-to-face. You can do just one, but it's ideal to share all four at once.

1. Something I love about you is _____.

2. Something I respect about you is _____.

3. Something I admire about you is _____.

4. Something I've learned from you (or would like to learn from you) is _____

_____.

♥ **4. Daily Dose of Awkward**

Physical contact is a vital part of any relationship. Even if you don't consider yourself a "touchy" person, our bodies and brains are wired for physical contact. This relationship hack can feel awkward even if you're already comfortable with physical affection, but the super-smart science people conducted the research, and the results are in: awkward contact makes good relationships even better.

Instructions: Choose from one of the awkward tasks below, or try all three. This exercise is best done daily for at least thirty days, but you can do it on whatever frequency makes sense for your relationship. Bonus points if you and your partner start laughing. Laughter releases an extra dose of feel-good brain juice on top of the benefits from the exercise itself.

1. Set a timer for two minutes, and make eye contact without talking or moving.
2. Set a timer for two minutes, and hug without talking or moving.
3. Kiss for six seconds.*

---

*The six-second kiss is a technique from the renowned Gottman Institute. "There doesn't have to be talking, listening, or problem-solving. It's just a time to connect with your partner physically and feel close to them. It also accomplishes a lot of principles and needs in our relationship in only six seconds. . . . A six second kiss is one of the least time-consuming ways to improve things with your partner. In fact, if you have two kisses per day the total time per week amounts to less than 90 seconds." From Kari Rusnak, LPC, CMHC, BC-TMH, "The Six Second Kiss," The Gottman Institute, https://www.gottman.com/blog/the-six-second-kiss.

 **Check-In**

Instructions: Either think about the following questions or write about them in your journal.

- Of those tasks listed, which ones were the easiest? Which were the hardest?
- Which ones do you think are the most useful for your relationship?
- What did you find difficult about doing these tasks?
- How are you doing with your daily practice?

Observation: One takeaway from this work is:

_____

Recommendation: Something I can do with this information is:

_____

The Four O's: Apologies Versus Amends

How often do you feel better when someone says the following to you?

- I'm sorry *if* you took that the wrong way.
- I'm sorry *if* you feel that way.
- I'm sorry *if* I did anything to make you upset.
- I'm sorry *if* you are too sensitive to take a joke.

I'm guessing the answer is never.

Saying "I'm sorry if . . ." has several problems:

- The word *I'm* focuses on the person who *caused* the rupture, not the person who was *harmed* by the rupture.

- The word *if* allows the person who caused the harm to bypass accountability.
- Saying "I'm sorry" doesn't offer any plan for preventing the same issue from recurring.
- Saying "I'm sorry" does not convey the desire to understand; it conveys the desire to be understood.

Saying "I'm sorry" is appropriate for minor things like forgetting to turn off the lights or if you accidentally bump into someone. Apologies are great for simple mistakes and basic human courtesy. But more severe relationship injuries need a higher-potency solution than an apology, which is where *making amends* comes into play. You do not need to struggle with addiction or be in a twelve-step program to make amends. I use a technique called the Four O's.*

What are the Four O's?

1. **Own** the thing you did. ("I admit that I _____.")

2. **Observe** how your behavior impacted the other person. ("I imagine you must have felt _____.")

3. **Outline** your plan not to do the thing again. ("In the future, I'll prevent this from happening again by _____.")

4. **Offer** to listen if your partner wants to share anything you missed. ("Is there anything else you need me to know about this? I'm willing to listen.")

👣 The Four O's of Relationship Repair

Instructions: After an argument—minor or large—take some time to think about the Four O's and use the following chart to write your script. Then share it with your partner. I've added an example to get you started.

---

*I based the Four O's technique on the twelve-step recovery principle of making amends. Steps 8 and 9 of the twelve-step model focus on making amends wherever possible, except when doing so would cause harm to self or others.

1	Own the Thing You Did ("I admit I . . .")

I admit I raised my voice during our argument.

2	Observe How Your Behavior Impacted Your Partner ("I imagine you must have felt . . .")

I imagine you must have felt angry, scared, confused, and overwhelmed.

3	Outline Your Plan Not to Do the Thing Again ("In the future, I'll prevent this from happening again by . . .")

In the future, I will make sure I am rested, fed, and emotionally ready to talk before bringing up something heavy.

4	Offer to Listen If They Need to Share Anything You Missed ("Is there anything else you need me to know about this? I'm willing to listen.")

Is there anything else about this situation you want me to know?

Preventing Relationship Ruptures

The next four tasks are preventative strategies so you can move through conflicts more smoothly. You'll learn how to use conflict languages, design a conflict contract, manage expectations, and use a confrontation script.

 ### 1. The Six Conflict Languages

You may have heard of Gary Chapman's book *The 5 Love Languages*, which describes different ways partners prefer to show and receive love and affection. The five love languages are as follows:

1. Words of affirmation
2. Acts of service
3. Quality time
4. Gifts
5. Physical affection

The 5 Love Languages is a useful tool for building intimacy, but relationships need to be just as fluent in the language of *conflict* as they are in the language of love. I've outlined six conflict languages to consider. When you know your conflict language, you lower the likelihood of volcanic relationship eruptions, and it's easier to safely maneuver through arguments when they arise.

Instructions: Read through each conflict language, and rank them in order of preference from one to six (with one being your top priority and six, your lowest). You can do this solo or share this task with your partner. If you and your partner have different conflict languages, you can discuss ways to compromise in the next task (conflict contracts).

GEOGRAPHIC LOCATION _____

The location of your arguments matters. Most experts advise against fighting in your bedroom. Wherever you decide to hold a heated discussion, it's best to sit or stand at least six feet away from each other. Why? Having physical space decreases the chances your nervous system will mistake your partner for a predator, so your logical brain is more likely to stay online. Arguments that occur in your car or in any location where you don't have space to walk away if necessary are not ideal.

Time Limits _____

It is useful to set time limits on arguments and take a break if things aren't resolved—even if the break means going to sleep angry. Just as our physical bodies need breaks and rest periods with exercise, our brains need breaks and rest periods during conflict. No one's brain can skillfully sustain the pace of hours-long marathon conflict sessions. Time limits prevent circular conversations from dragging on all night.

Format (Digital Versus In-Person) _____

Arguing over the phone or via text is not recommended, but discussing heated topics over video chat can be a useful hack for preventing escalation. Some people feel safer engaging in conflict without the person in their physical space. Others feel safer when they can see the person's body language. Some people don't care either way. You can try both to see how your system responds to each format.

Emergency Exit Strategy _____

Sometimes arguments need to be immediately halted, especially if you or your partner is unable to maintain your emotional grounding. Choosing a safe word ahead of time is a way to access an emergency exit during a conflict. When either of you deploys the word during a conflict, you both agree to immediately cease and take a one-hour break.

Time of Day _____

Because many of us never learned how to negotiate conflict skillfully, we often jump right into conversations without considering the time of day. Some people identify as morning people, but for others, trying to skillfully manage a conflict before coffee is a really bad call. Some people are exhausted when they come home from work and need time to decompress before addressing relationship issues. Some people feel lethargic and foggy in the afternoon. Knowing your brain's patterns is a less-talked-about but very useful mindfulness tool.

FOOD FIGHTS _____

Some people can't imagine trying to have a difficult conversation while trying to eat. For others, sitting down over a meal or a cup of coffee is a way to maintain regulation during arguments. It is hard to lose your temper and scream while smelling, chewing, tasting, and swallowing food. Saving high-intensity conversations for mealtime is a useful strategy for some people in some situations.

Now that you've had time to consider your conflict language (and hopefully your partner has participated, although this isn't a requirement), you'll create an agreement for you and your partner to use during conflict.

2. Conflict Contract

You don't buy a house, join a gym, or sign up for a cell phone plan without a contract. Yet unless people land in divorce court, the idea of a contract or agreement in a relationship is never discussed. This task invites you and your partner to create a conflict contract, which is a set of predetermined rules that you agree to follow during arguments. This technique won't prevent conflict, but it will minimize huge eruptions and unnecessary relationship dings.

Instructions: Complete the conflict contract with your partner(s), discussing what makes the most sense for your relationship. Then take a photo of your responses. If a conflict arises in the relationship, immediately take out your conflict contract. If one of you is unable or unwilling to follow the contract guidelines, immediately pause and take a break. Wait at least thirty minutes before trying again.

OUR CONFLICT CONTRACT

During an argument, we, _____ and _____

[insert your names], agree to the following terms:

Fights will last no longer than _____ minutes.

If we cannot resolve the argument in this time frame, we will break for _____ minutes.

During the break, each of us agrees to go to _____

and _____ to cool down.

During a conflict, we agree to stand no closer than _____ feet to each other.

The room where we agree to have our argument is _____.

If we are not at home, we will go to _____ to have our discussion.

During a conflict, one partner will sit _____

and the other will sit _____.

▸ During arguments, it is acceptable to leave the house.

  Y/N

▸ During arguments, it is acceptable to yell.

  Y/N

▸ During arguments, it is acceptable to name-call.

  Y/N

▸ During arguments, it is acceptable to threaten to end the relationship.

  Y/N

▸ During arguments, it is acceptable to have our conversation in front of the kids.

  Y/N

▸ During arguments, it is acceptable to bring up issues from the past.

  Y/N

▸ During arguments, it is acceptable to interrupt the other.

  Y/N

▸ During arguments, it is acceptable to say generalized things like "You always . . ." or "You never . . ."

  Y/N

▸ If an argument is unresolved at night, it is okay to go to sleep and try again in the morning.

  Y/N *(Note: The answer to this one for everyone should ideally be yes.)*

▸ It is acceptable to talk to family members about our argument.

Y/N

Add any other rules, agreements, or guidelines you want in the space below:

_____

_____

_____

SIGNED

_____

_____

DATE

_____

3. Expectations Management

Instructions: Fill in the chart. If you need more space, copy the chart into your journal. If your partner is willing to join you in this exercise, fantastic. If not, you can still reflect on your expectations and either adjust them or seek out a helpful resource to help you navigate.

Topic	My Expectations About This Topic	Have I Shared This with My Partner?	My Partner's Expectations About This Topic Are	What's a Compromise We Can Agree to Try?	If We Can't Agree on a Compromise, What's One Resource We Can Use to Help Us?
Sex		Y/N			

Topic	My Expectations About This Topic	Have I Shared This with My Partner?	My Partner's Expectations About This Topic Are	What's a Compromise We Can Agree to Try?	If We Can't Agree on a Compromise, What's One Resource We Can Use to Help Us?
Money		Y/N			
Parenting		Y/N			
Family/ in-laws		Y/N			
Time		Y/N			
Household chores		Y/N			

4. Using a Five-Step Confrontation Script

No one enjoys being asked "why" questions. Asking why questions of your children, friends, partner, or colleague implies from the start that *you* are right and *they* are wrong. The word *why* is loaded with shame and immediately sets up the conversation for failure. The climate of the conversation shifts from collaborative to defensive.

Instructions: Instead of asking, "Why did you do that?" try using this five-step script* when you want to confront someone. You can read right from the script to your partner, or you can write down the script and then share it with them.

---

* "What I make up about that is" is adapted from Pia Mellody's talking boundary format used by the Meadows.

CONFRONTATION SCRIPT

Step 1: "I noticed you did/said/didn't do _____."

Step 2: "What I make up about that is _____."

Step 3: "Right now, I'm feeling _____."

Step 4: "What I'd like from you is _____."

Step 5: "Are you willing to discuss this?"

It is important to take these steps in order and *not* to deviate from the script. Speaking from the vantage point of *observer* or *interpreter* rather than *accuser* makes it more likely that the person to whom you are speaking can hear you without spiraling. The "are you willing" part of the script creates space for *consent* because skillful confrontation is difficult when the person you want to confront feels ambushed. Disclaimer: This is an odd way of speaking, and every client to whom I've given this script feels ridiculous using it. But remember, if the "normal" way of confronting people worked, it would have worked by now.

Four Relationship Myths

Some of the biggest barriers to healthy relationships are the misinformation and myths that circulate, creating chaos and confusion. This next section helps dismantle the relationship myths that keep many of us feeling stuck and confused.

♥ Four Relationship Myths Keeping You Stuck

Instructions: Read through each relationship myth. Then, either think about the reflection questions, write your answers in the chart, or copy the chart into your journal if you need more space. I've provided an example in the first myth to get you started.

Myth 1: Never Go to Sleep Angry

Why it's a myth: The saying "never go to sleep angry" is *not* good advice because it ignores the reality of your brain's design. Trying to stay mindful, present, empathetic, skillful, and considerate is difficult enough during an argument without adding sleep deprivation to the mix.

REFLECTION QUESTIONS

Where Did I Learn to Never Go to Sleep Angry?	What Is My Core Fear or Belief Driving My Desire to Stay Awake?	What Is One Way I Can Tend to My Fears?	What Is One Request I Can Make of My Partner to Tend to My Fears?
This piece of advice comes from a Bible verse. It is a lovely idea but not always practical.	I'm afraid that if I go to sleep angry, either my partner or I will die during the night or that they will leave me.	I can remind myself that a sleep-deprived brain is unlikely to stay logical, and that it's less likely I will say hurtful things if I get some rest. I also can remind myself that although anything is possible, it's unlikely that we will not be alive in the morning to finish the conversation.	I can ask my partner if they're willing to hug before we go to sleep, even if we're angry.

Myth 2: You Should Spend Every Waking Moment with Your Partner

Why it's a myth: Healthy relationships require you to continue to maintain separate identities from each other. If you spend every waking moment with your partner, you will not have the time or space to cultivate friendships or interests outside of the relationship.

REFLECTION QUESTIONS

Where Did I Learn That I Need to Spend All My Time with My Partner?	What Is My Core Fear or Belief Driving My Desire to Spend All My Time with My Partner?	What Is One Way I Can Tend to My Fears?	What Is One Request I Can Make of My Partner to Tend to My Fears?

Myth 3: Your Partner Is Supposed to Take Care of All Your Needs

Why it's a myth: As an adult person, you want to be and have a partner, not a parent. Anytime you feel more like a parent than a partner, or anytime you expect your partner to be a surrogate parent for you, resentment is sure to follow.

REFLECTION QUESTIONS

Where Did I Learn That My Partner Is Supposed to Meet All My Needs?	What Is My Core Fear If My Partner Doesn't Take Care of All My Needs?	What Is One Way I Can Self-Parent When My Partner Isn't Available?	What Is One Request I Can Make of My Partner to Help Me in This Area?

Myth 4: Relationships Require You to Extend Unconditional Love

Why it's a myth: The *feeling* or spiritual principle of unconditional love is always a valid choice, but *extending* unconditional love is different. All adult relationships require conditions to be healthy. The only relationships in which it is appropriate to extend unconditional love is with children and animals.

REFLECTION QUESTIONS

Where Did I Learn That Relationships Require Unconditional Love?	What Is My Core Fear or Belief About Unconditional Love?	What Is One Way I Can Tend to My Fears?	What Is One Request I Can Make of My Friends or Family to Help Me?

 Check-In

Instructions: Either think about the following questions or write about them in your journal.

▸ Which of the tasks was easiest for you? Which was the most difficult?

▸ If you skipped over any tasks, consider going back to try doing them.

▸ What surprised you about doing this kind of relationship-skill-building work?

▸ If your partner was willing, how was your experience collaborating with them on the tasks?

▸ If your partner was not willing, how are you feeling about doing this work solo? Are there any other resources available to help you feel supported?

▸ How are you doing with your daily practice?

Observation: One takeaway from this work is:

_____

Recommendation: Something I can do with this information is:

_____

Boundaries and Codependency

In *Daring Greatly*, Dr. Brené Brown teaches that "Connection is why we're here. We are hardwired to connect with others, it's what gives purpose and meaning to our lives, and without it there is suffering."

It's true that the absence of connection leads to the presence of suffering, but it is vital to add one big caveat: connection at all costs is *codependency*. To be clear, I'm not a big fan of the word *codependent*. It can be blame-y and shame-y, and the word makes it seem like we don't need other people. But until we have a better name for the phenomenon, *codependent* is likely to stick around. The next section focuses on recognizing codependency—and what you can do about it.

What Is Codependency?

Codependency is defined as "a psychological condition or a relationship in which a person manifesting low self-esteem and a strong desire for approval has an unhealthy attachment to another often controlling or manipulative person (such as a person with an addiction to alcohol or drugs)."*

---

*Putting others' needs before your own isn't always codependency. There are times in every healthy relationship when sacrifices and compromises need to be made. From "Codependency," *Merriam-Webster Dictionary*, Merriam-Webster, https://www.merriam-webster.com/dictionary/codependency.

That definition is a bit wordy. I define codependency like this:

🔑 **Codependency: The thing that happens when we become so obsessed with someone *else's* life that we completely neglect *our own*.**

People who fall on the caretaking side of codependency often feel like they're providing love and support. You might wonder, *But aren't I supposed to be helpful and supportive and caring toward the people I love?*

Fair question. It's helpful to recognize the difference between care*taking* and care*giving*:

🔑 **Caretaking: When you do for someone what they *could* or *should* be doing for themselves. The message of caretaking is, "You are not capable."**

🔑 **Caregiving: When you help someone who needs help. The message of caregiving is, "You are not alone."**

Codependency falls under the category of *process addiction*. A process addiction is like a chemical addiction, but instead of ingesting a substance, you hyperfocus on either a person or a behavior. The outward focus interferes with your ability to take care of your *own* needs and eventually compromises your health. Psychologist Joaquín Selva writes: "Modern understandings of codependency now refer to 'a specific relationship addiction characterized by preoccupation and extreme dependence—emotional, social and sometimes physical—on another person.'"[*]

Like all addictions, codependency is not a character flaw but a suboptimal way our system tries to protect us from pain. (See part 1 on addictions and habits.) A few (but not all) reasons you might get stuck in codependent relationships include the following:

---

[*]Joaquín Selva, Bc.S., "Codependency: What Are the Signs and How to Overcome It," PositivePsychology.com, February 9, 2018, https://positivepsychology.com/codependency-definition-signs-worksheets.

- Codependent patterns in your family of origin
- Overprotective or underprotective caregivers in childhood
- Fear of abandonment
- Fear of loneliness
- Fear of losing people you love
- Feelings of unworthiness
- Feeling guilty all the time

🪷 Do You Have Codependent Tendencies?

Instructions: Read the codependency indicators in the chart below. Write T for true or F for false next to each one.

Codependency Assessment	T/F
1. I am usually the caretaker in relationships.	
2. I tend to work harder in relationships than the other person.	
3. I feel burned out in relationships.	
4. I feel resentful in my relationships.	
5. I have trouble asking for my needs.	
6. I have trouble setting boundaries.	
7. I feel guilty if I take time for myself.	
8. I tolerate mistreatment from people.	
9. I am afraid of being rejected or abandoned.	
10. I'm afraid of conflict.	
11. I feel unlovable.	
12. I feel like other people's needs matter more than mine.	
13. I feel frustrated when other people don't take my advice or want my help.	
14. I tend to attract needy people.	
15. I try to protect other people from experiencing consequences or pain.	

Codependency Assessment	T/F
16. I need constant reassurance.	
17. I blame myself for causing problems for other people.	
18. I feel like I need to be a parent to my partner.	
19. I am afraid of being alone.	
20. I make excuses for other people's behavior.	

Scoring: Count the total number of your "true" responses, and see the corresponding point range below.

If you marked true for:

One to five: mild codependent tendencies: Your skills are gold-star level, and you can confidently skip the next section.

Six to ten: moderate codependent tendencies: Codependency might not be your biggest challenge, but you'll likely benefit from sharpening your skills. Proceed to the next section.

Eleven to fifteen: high codependent tendencies: Codependency is actively interfering with your ability to live your best life, and you are likely resentful, frustrated, and feeling edgy by your efforts to manage relationships. The next section gives you important information.

Sixteen to twenty: extreme codependent tendencies: If you fall into this category, you're feeling overwhelmed, exhausted, confused, afraid, stuck, stressed out, and unsure that things can possibly get better. The next section gives you important information, and it might be useful to supplement with other resources (see Suggested Reading) or therapy if that's an option.

Healthy relationships give you energy and move you toward your authentic self. Codependent relationships drain your energy and take you away from your authentic self. As author Dennis Merritt Jones put it, "It feels good to be accepted, loved and approved by others, but often the membership fee to belong to that club is far too high of a price to pay." When the only currency of connection is helping, you eventually believe that your only value comes from what you *do* rather than who you *are*.

♥ Journal Prompt: Codependency Recovery

Instructions: Consider these questions. Either think about them or write them down in your journal.

1. What did I learn in my family of origin about having needs?
2. What did I learn in my family of origin about taking care of other people's needs?
3. What do I want to believe about having needs?
4. What would need to change in my life if I valued my own needs?
5. What am I afraid would happen if I started valuing my own needs?

Boundaries: The Antidote to Codependency

Boundaries are the antidote to codependency. Like most mental health trends in the zeitgeist, the word *boundaries* is misused and misunderstood. The next section clarifies what boundaries are—and what they're not. The most common confusion around boundaries is mistaking a *boundary* for a *request*.

Boundaries Versus Requests

- **Request:** When you ask someone to do (or not to do) something. The power to say yes or no lies with *them*.
- **Boundary:** What you choose to do in response to someone else's behavior. The power to say yes or no lies with *you*.

Request	Boundary
Please do not call me after eight P.M.	I do not answer calls after eight P.M. If you choose to call me after eight P.M., I will not pick up the phone.
Please don't have more than two cocktails at the party.	If you choose to have more than two cocktails, I will choose to leave.

Request	Boundary
I would really prefer if you didn't bring up politics at dinner.	If you choose to bring up politics at dinner, I will remove myself from the table.
I don't like it when you yell. I would like you not to raise your voice when we argue.	If you choose to raise your voice during an argument, I will choose to remove myself from the conversation until we can speak to each other calmly.

This is usually the point when people frown and say, "Boundaries sound an awful lot like ultimatums. I don't like the sound of this."

I hear you. Boundaries and ultimatums may seem similar, but they are not the same:

ⲟ━O Ultimatums are about power, control, and relationship *domination*.

ⲟ━O Boundaries are about safety, containment, and relationship *preservation*.

If you're not sure whether you are setting a boundary or laying down an ultimatum, ask yourself if your intention is to control your partner or to preserve your relationship. Big difference. Boundaries are intended to create conditions for psychological safety, not to interfere with someone's behavior. The beautiful thing about boundaries is that they never need to be validated, understood, or even accepted. The full power of holding or not holding boundaries lies in your hands and your hands only.

A note about "crossing boundaries": Because *boundary* is just a fancy word for "choice," it's crucial to remember that *no one* can cross your boundaries. A boundary is a choice *you* make, and it is a line *you* hold. People might test you, nag you, or guilt you into dropping your boundaries, but the only person who can cross your boundaries is *you*. If you try to implement a boundary (aka "make a choice") and someone invades your space or prohibits you from making that choice, that is not "boundary crossing"—that is abuse.

💭 Journal Prompt: My Boundary Beliefs

Instructions: Consider the following questions. Either think about them or write down your thoughts in your journal.

1. What, if anything, did my family teach about boundaries? Did their behavior match their words?
2. What do I believe about boundaries?
3. What do I *want* to believe about boundaries?

Now that you've explored your codependent tendencies, examined your beliefs about needs, and clarified the difference between boundaries and requests, the next section lays out six types of boundaries.

👣 Six Types of Boundaries—and How to Get Them to Stick

Instructions: You don't have to overload your system by trying to do all of these at the same time. Don't start with the boundary that is most important to you; start with whatever boundary is easiest for you before you attempt the more difficult ones.

1. Confrontation boundaries
2. Sleep boundaries
3. Transition boundaries
4. Listening boundaries
5. Conversational boundaries
6. Time boundaries

1. Confrontation Boundaries

Why they matter: Using a structure for a confrontation promotes safety. Creating a *structure* for confrontation is necessary to contain the *content* of a confrontation. Without it, feelings tend to fly around unskillfully.

How to set them: Use a confrontation script. Anytime you need to confront someone, use the following script. It may feel odd to speak in this way, but remember, if the "normal" way worked, it would have worked by now.

Step 1: I heard you say/saw you do _____.

Step 2: I interpretated that to mean _____.

Step 3: Right now I'm feeling _____.

Step 4: What I'd like to request from you is _____.

Step 5: Are you willing?

> *If they are willing to honor your request, you can stop here. If they are not willing to honor your request, you have the option of adding the following step:*

Step 6: I respect your right to make your choices. Because you are choosing _____

_____, my boundary is _____.

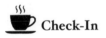 **Check-In**

Instructions: Either think about the following questions or write about them in your journal.

  ▸ Did you try setting confrontation boundaries?
  ▸ If not, why? If so, how did it turn out?

Observation: One takeaway from this work is:

_____

Recommendation: Something I can do with this information is:

_____

2. Sleep Boundaries

Why they matter: All humans need sleep. Our brains work better, our minds are clearer, and our bodies function better when we get adequate sleep. There are times when adequate sleep is legitimately impossible (especially if you have infants), but whenever you have the choice to set sleep boundaries, I highly encourage you to consider implementing the following.

How to set them: Sleep in separate spaces. Sleeping in separate rooms (if this is an option) is one of the most effective ways to ensure you get adequate sleep. Sleeping in separate rooms is also culturally frowned upon and is often referred to as "sleep divorce." I cannot tell you how many people are terrified that if they sleep separately, inevitably they will end up divorced or split. But just because it's "normal" for couples to sleep in the same bed doesn't mean it's optimal. A good night's sleep separately is *far* better for your relationship than a restless night of semi-consciousness together.

If you have the option of sleeping in separate bedrooms, try it for thirty days and see how you feel. If this is not an option, consider alternating days in the bedroom and on the couch or blow-up mattress. Everyone pushes back on this suggestion initially, and everyone with a partner who snores, stays up late, goes to sleep early, makes noise, or tosses and turns later reports that the separate space is immensely helpful.

Check-In

Instructions: Either think about the following questions or write about them in your journal.

- ▸ Did you try setting sleep boundaries?
- ▸ If not, why? If so, how did it turn out?

Observation: One takeaway from this work is:

_____

Recommendation: Something I can do with this information is:

_____

3. Transition Boundaries

Why they matter: All too often, we storm through our lives without mindfully transitioning between tasks. We wake up to screaming children, stare at screens until we're asleep, and rush around going to and from work without stopping to take a breath. Transition boundaries don't take a lot of time, they don't cost any money, and they can be powerful hacks for feeling more in control of your life.

How to set them: Create ambush-free zones. To create these zones, you and your partner agree not to talk to each other for a minimum of ten minutes when you get home. If you work from home, then you agree not to talk to each other for ten minutes when you are finished with your workday. The same goes for first thing in the morning. For at least ten minutes after you wake up (preferably thirty, but ten still gets the job done), *do not* talk to each other. Use that time to catch your breath, stretch, and defog your head before launching into the day's to-do list.

 Check-In

Instructions: Either think about the following questions or write about them in your journal.

- ▸ Did you try setting transition boundaries?
- ▸ If not, why? If so, how did it turn out?

Observation: One takeaway from this work is:

_____

Recommendation: Something I can do with this information is:

_____

4. Listening Boundaries

Why they matter: If we don't skillfully listen to our partners, it is unlikely that they will feel loved and secure in the relationship. How you *receive* information is just as important to your relationship as how you *transmit* information.

How to set them: Hold space instead of giving advice. Holding space means listening without judgment. It means compassionately staying with someone in their reality without trying to change it. As a skillful space holder, you help your partner hear *their* voice rather than trying to make them listen to yours. A good way to practice holding space is to use reflective listening. To practice reflective listening, each partner sets a timer for fifteen minutes. One partner is the "sender" and one is the "receiver." The sender needs to use very short sentences so the receiver can fully absorb them. You can use this script to practice:

Step 1: What I heard you say was _____

_____.

Step 2: Is that right? [Your partner will either say yes or clarify what they were saying.]

Step 3: Okay, I think I understand now. What you're saying is _____

_____.

Step 4: Is that right? [If they say yes, continue.]

Step 5: That makes sense. What would help you feel more supported right now?

☕ Check-In

Instructions: Either think about the following questions or write about them in your journal.

- ▸ Did you try setting listening boundaries?
- ▸ If not, why? If so, how did it turn out?

Observation: One takeaway from this work is:

_____

Recommendation: Something I can do with this information is:

_____

5. Conversational Boundaries

Why they matter: Certain conversations are hard but necessary—finances, sexual expectations, and parenting, to name a few. But other conversations are completely unnecessary—having yet *another* Thanksgiving debate with your uncle Keith about the reality of climate change is almost always a waste of your time and energy.

How to set them: Decide which conversations are fully off-limits. This often includes subjects such as politics and religion but can include any topics you are unwilling to discuss. I've added an example to the following chart to get you started. Complete the rest of the chart, and if the topic comes up, you can politely say, "That's a conversation I'm unwilling to have."

Person in My Life	Conversations I'm Unwilling to Have
Parents	Religion, politics, how I spend money, my parenting choices
Aunts or uncles	My medical choices

Check-In

Instructions: Either think about the following questions or write about them in your journal.

▸ Did you try setting conversational boundaries?

▸ If not, why? If so, how did it turn out?

Observation: One takeaway from this work is:

_____

Recommendation: Something I can do with this information is:

_____

6. Time Boundaries

Why they matter: If your time is without boundaries, you'll likely end up feeling burned out, resentful, frustrated, and exhausted.

How to set them: Pick a start time and a stop time for conversations, outings, activities—and set a timer. Time boundaries can be five hours to attend an event or five minutes to catch up with a friend. The trick to keeping time boundaries is to tell your friend, spouse, or family *ahead* of time so there are no surprises.

Common Objections to Setting Boundaries

What if I try to set boundaries and the person gets mad?

It is likely that *some* people will have a problem with your boundaries. Remind yourself that when people get angry about your boundaries, that's a sign that boundaries are, in fact, necessary with those people. Healthy and safe people will honor your boundaries, not punish you for setting them.

What if I lose the relationship?

If you lose the relationship after setting healthy and appropriate boundaries, what kind of relationship did you have to begin with?

Why should I have to do this? Why can't people just be decent and reasonable and read my mind?

I absolutely get this objection and agree. It would be much easier if people did what they should do (and if they did what we wanted them to do), but waiting for people to do (or not do) things is a surefire way to build resentment. Remind yourself that you don't *have* to set boundaries, but if you don't, the feelings of resentment and frustration are going to be *yours* to manage.

Conclusion: Codependence Versus Interdependence

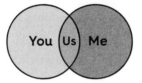

All relationships require times when one person gives and the other takes—it is wholly unrealistic to expect otherwise. But the opposite of codependence is *not* independence. Complete isolation from the world and refusal to acknowledge the importance of relationships are different expressions of the same problem. Rather than independence, the opposite of codependence is *interdependence*.

In an interdependent relationship, there is both overlap of and differentiation between partners (or between a person and their group or community). An article on Psych Central* highlights several characteristics of interdependent relationships. These include the following:

- ▸ Clearly defined and respected boundaries
- ▸ Individuality in thoughts, beliefs, and pursuits

*Kurt Smith, PsyD, LMFT, LPCC, AFC, "Codependency vs. Interdependency," Psych Central, May 20, 2022, https://psychcentral.com/lib/codependency-vs-interdependency#interdependence.

▸ A continual effort to practice healthy communication and respect for each other

▸ A sense of security in your ability to strengthen the relationship or work with the other to face relationship challenges

For people who struggle to shift from codependence to interdependence, twelve-step groups such as Co-Dependents Anonymous (CoDA) provide free tools, meetings, and resources.* The qualities of interdependence are noted in the following recovery affirmations listed on the CoDA website:†

▸ I acknowledge I sometimes need the help of others.

▸ I am aware of painful feelings and express them appropriately.

▸ I meet my own needs and wants when possible. I reach out for help when it's necessary and appropriate.

▸ I am committed to my safety and leave situations that feel unsafe or are inconsistent with my goals.

▸ I am rooted in my own values, even if others don't agree or become angry.

▸ I value the opinions of those I trust, without needing to gain their approval.

Sometimes people worry that they will be heartless and cold as they move away from codependence. It's necessary to remind yourself that not only is it possible for compassion to coexist with boundaries, but it's also essential to staying healthy.

🔑 **Compassion with boundaries allows us to maintain connection with our Self.**

---

*Some twelve-step groups are wonderful, but many are cultlike. Moreover, I do not subscribe to the religious and shaming language. If you choose to participate in a twelve-step-based recovery group, proceed with optimistic caution.

†"Recovery Patterns of Codependence," Co-Dependents Anonymous, https://coda.org/meeting-materials/patterns -of-recovery. Disclaimer: There are many problems with the twelve-step model and with the definition of *codependency*, because it is a term often used to shame people at the expense of understanding behavioral functionality.

⌐O Compassion without boundaries leads to disconnection and self-betrayal.

⌐O Bottom-Line Takeaways

1. The human brain is not wired for modern dating.
2. When you meet someone new, your brain gets drunk.
3. Breakups can create physical discomfort.
4. Couples work is not recommended if there is abuse in the relationship.
5. Making amends is preferable to offering apologies.
6. Knowing your conflict language can prevent fights from escalating.
7. "Never go to sleep angry" is a total myth. Hard conversations require rested brains.
8. Codependency is when you obsess about someone else's life at the expense of your own.
9. Boundaries are the solution to codependency.
10. Ultimatums are about relationship domination; boundaries are about relationship preservation.

DOS AND DON'TS OF CREATING SKILLFUL RELATIONSHIPS

Do	Don't
Use the Four O's for relationship repair.	Say "I'm sorry."
Take the time to manage expectations in your relationships.	Expect your partner to read your mind.
Remember that boundaries are the antidote to codependency.	Think that boundaries are mean. They may not feel kind, but boundaries protect relationships.
Remind yourself that the human brain is not wired for modern dating.	Go on marathon dates and expect your brain to be able to make rational decisions.

End-of-Level Challenge

You are much more likely to avoid turbulence in friendships and intimate relationships if you shift your focus from the primary relationship to something else in your life. Fill in the following chart slices with other people, places, thoughts, or things that you can go to to help take the pressure off your primary relationships.

Bonus challenge: Color in the mandala. Coloring is good for your nervous system.

Congratulations! You've reached the end of this part. Use the space on the next page for final observations and recommendations:

Observations:

_____

_____

_____

Recommendations:

_____

_____

_____

PART 4

Decluttering Your Inner Closets

A Compassionate Approach to Self-Awareness

This part tackles the stuff we *all* have hidden in our psychological closets. You'll explore why self-compassion is a key part of the change process, how to deal with annoying feelings, and what to do when "doing the work" doesn't get you anywhere.

Hiding from the monsters only made them stronger.

—C. L. Wilson, *Crown of Crystal Flame*

n our efforts to minimize discomfort, we scroll through countless articles. We watch peppy TikTokers teach about positive parenting. We pretend to love cauliflower rice.* We earnestly try to be good parents, friends, and humans. Nevertheless . . . meaningful and happy lives remain elusive.

It's tempting to believe that if we possess enough money, beauty, and kitchen gadgetry, we can evolve beyond the discomfort of being human. But as Dr. Susan David said in her brilliant TED Talk, "Discomfort is the price of admission to a meaningful life."

What are we missing?

In our efforts to be "good people" or "happy people," we miss out on being *whole* people. Wholeness, defined as the state of being complete or in harmony, is necessary to know who we are and what we want. Health cannot fully exist without wholeness—the linguistic root of the word *health* is the word *whole*. We are quick to think that if we find happiness, we'll finally feel whole. But wholeness is the antecedent to happiness, not the other way around.

⚷ Wholeness is the mother of happiness.

Wholeness (and its birth child, happiness) becomes more readily available when you gather and organize the tangled mess hidden in your psychological closets. This part helps make this process less overwhelming. If you're unsure if this type of work is necessary, here are two assessments to see if this material is relevant for you.

💭 Assessment 1: Emotion-Avoidance Inventory

Instructions: Fill in the blanks of the following chart. If the middle column remains empty (it won't), feel free to skip this chapter.

---

* Our relationship with food should resemble a loving parent feeding a child, not a critical parent punishing a child. Any approach to eating that values outcome over process has the potential to be toxic.

Uncomfortable Emotion	Something You Have Done to Avoid This Emotion	What Was the Result?
Sadness		
Shame		
Anger		
Fear		
Loneliness		

Assessment 2: Reality-Avoidance Inventory

Instructions: Fill in the following chart. I've added an example to get you started. Remind yourself that this exercise is going to be uncomfortable. Hold your nose, close your eyes, and jump. Do not shame yourself for what you discover. If this exercise becomes too painful or if you feel overwhelmed, immediately put down this book and take a break.

Reality I Don't Want to Accept	Things I Do to Avoid This Reality	What Are the Consequences of Avoiding This Reality?
I cannot force my partner to stop drinking.	Nag, plead, beg, threaten, scream, bargain, enable, and abandon my own needs.	Resentment, exhaustion, and depression.

Reality I Don't Want to Accept	Things I Do to Avoid This Reality	What Are the Consequences of Avoiding This Reality?

Our best efforts to avoid our internal mess often generate an even greater external mess. As author and psychiatrist R. D. Laing put it, "Pain in this life is not avoidable, but the pain we create avoiding pain is avoidable." Avoiding pain is a form of self-deception. Economist Russ Roberts noted, "Self-deception can be more comforting than self-knowledge. We like to fool ourselves." We all have things about ourselves, and our lives, that we *know* to be true that we don't *want* to be true. Read that sentence again. As author Patrick Rothfuss put it, "There are times when the mind is dealt such a blow it hides itself in insanity. While this may not seem beneficial, it is. There are times when reality is nothing but pain, and to escape that pain the mind must leave reality behind." The following list contains some uncomfortable truths that most people—including me—perform psychological contortion to avoid.

UNCOMFORTABLE TRUTHS

- There will never be enough time to do everything you want to do.
- You will be misunderstood.
- People will not always love you the way you want to be loved.
- People will do stupid things and cause harm to themselves—and to you.

- You will not be the best at everything.
- Pain is usually required before we're willing to change.
- Not all relationships can be repaired.
- Love is not always enough.
- You cannot control other people.
- Some people will always take advantage of your generosity.
- To get good at anything, you'll need to be bad at it first.
- You will never be perfect.

Although this information sounds like an epic bummer, remind yourself that "the cave you fear to enter holds the treasure you seek."* Valuable things often hide in unlikely places. We often search for happiness in the things we buy, the food we eat, and in the relationships we chase. But trying to extract happiness from our external environment doesn't work. If it did, every rich, fit, beautiful, or successful person would be blissfully happy—and as anyone who ever secretly binged *Bling Empire*, *The Real Housewives*, or *Selling Sunset* knows, they aren't. As author Martha Beck put it, "To live a life that's wrong for you is a form of dying. There are people who have lives that look perfect. They try to be happy, they believe they should be happy . . . but if it's off course from their north star, they aren't satisfied."

❀ Journal Prompt: The Happiness Trap

Instructions: You can use these prompts to write your thoughts in your journal, but if you don't want to write, you can simply think about the questions.

- Think of a person you believed would make you happy. How did that work out?
- Think of a place you hoped would make you happy. Did the happiness last?
- Think of a thing you bought that you thought would make you happy. What happened?

---

*This line is often attributed to Carl Jung, but there is some debate about whether he actually said these exact words.

As you read earlier, if you want to feel happy, you'll first need to feel whole. Self-awareness is the door to wholeness. But there's a slight problem. The process of becoming self-aware is a messy one. In *The Secret Life of Bees*, Sue Monk Kidd writes: "Knowing can be a curse on a person's life. I'd traded in a pack of lies for a pack of truth, and I didn't know which one was heavier . . . once you know the truth, you can't ever go back and pick up your suitcase of lies. Heavier or not, the truth is yours now." The ability to tolerate your truth is the key to unlocking self-awareness. Self-awareness requires you not only to acknowledge life's uncomfortable truths but also to venture into the dark maze of your mind, a practice known as *shadow work* (popularized by Carl Jung).*

WHAT IS SHADOW WORK?

In the physical realm, shadows are created when light is blocked. Psychological shadows are created when *awareness* is blocked. We all have qualities about ourselves that make us cringe. We all have stories we would never dream of sharing. Have you ever had a thought stroll across your mind that made you go, "Yikes. That couldn't have been *me* who just thought that!" Have you ever felt guilty because you secretly felt jealous of a friend's

---

* Many Indigenous cultures practice shadow work (by many different names), and Carl Jung was certainly not the first person to discover the benefits of entering the unknown spaces in the psyche.

success? That's your shadow. "Shadow work" sounds super woo and mystical, but it's simply a metaphor for knowing all aspects of yourself. The more access you have to your mind, the more space you can create for consciously *responding* to life rather than unconsciously *reacting* to it. Hindu sage and teacher Ramana Maharshi offered a compelling reason to do this work when he wrote: "Your own Self-Realization is the greatest service you can render the world."

Checklist: Will Shadow Work Help Me?

Instructions: Put a check mark next to any statements that describe you. If you check one or more statements on this list, you may find shadow work useful.

	You overreact to little things.
	You are confused why certain things bother you more than other people.
	You can't remember the last time you laughed.
	You feel guilty all the time.
	You feel angry all the time.
	You notice yourself judging other people.
	You find yourself repeating relationship patterns.
	Your behavior causes you to think, "Why did I do that?"
	You are afraid what you might discover if you go inside your mind.
	You tend to avoid conflict.

Psychologist and author Brandon Goleman made the phrase *emotional intelligence* (EQ) part of the zeitgeist. EQ is the degree to which you can identify, contain, and express your emotional truth. Shadow intelligence (SQ) is the degree to which you can identify, befriend, and skillfully manage your psychological truth, no matter how messy. EQ is necessary to achieve success. SQ is necessary to *enjoy* your success without shame or resistance.

🔑 **An important disclaimer about shadow work before you continue:**

This material is intended to familiarize you with and introduce you to shadow work concepts. It is not intended to be a deep dive or to replace therapy. If you are troubled by thoughts of self-harm or harm to others, if you are currently in crisis, or if in any way this work makes you feel unsafe, skip this section and return to it with the guidance of a trained mental health professional.

🔑 **Another disclaimer about shadow work before you continue:**

Like everything, shadow work also has a shadow side. It's tempting to go nutty bananas overspiritualizing things that can be taken at face value. Not everything is necessarily a "sign." Not everything needs to have a deeper meaning. Pithy social media posts often fail to recognize complexity and attribute external circumstances to internal problems. Examples of shadow work axioms that may sometimes be true but are certainly not universal include the following:

▸ "Anything that bothers you about someone else is a quality about yourself you don't like." (*Not always true. Sometimes what bothers you about someone else is that they are objectively acting like a prat.*)

▸ "Your thoughts create your reality." (*Not always true. Your reality also is created by genetics, geopolitical unrest, family of origin, privilege, and access to things like health care and a living wage.*)

▸ "If you're suffering, it's because you manifested the situation." (*Not always true. There's that pesky problem of other people having free will.*)

▸ "If you're upset with someone, it's only because you're projecting your unhealed trauma onto them." (*Not always true. If they are causing harm to you or to someone else, it's reasonable to be upset.*)

▸ "What people say about you has everything to do with them and nothing to do with you." (*Not always true. Everyone, including you and me, occasionally acts in less-than-ideal ways, and constructive criticism is warranted in those situations.*)

We don't want to be so open-minded that our brains fall out.* As you traverse the path of self-awareness, remember that there are many reasons why people trigger you besides your shadow.

Five Reasons Someone Might Trigger You

1. They possess qualities you desire to have.
2. They are doing things you want to do.
3. They remind you of someone else.
4. You're hangry.
5. They're jerks.

⚷ A final disclaimer: Sometimes we think we need shadow work when the situation calls for *trauma* work. How can you tell the difference? Shadow work is often uncomfortable and unpleasant, but it should *never* feel unsafe.

With those caveats in place, let's continue.

---

* The author of this statement is unknown. I've seen it attributed to Carl Jung, Carl Sagan, Richard Feynman, and G. K. Chesterton.

Whose Lie Is It Anyway?

To start living, we need to stop lying.

Can you honestly say you *never* lie? The word *liar* conjures up images of the Tinder swindler, corrupt politicians, and miracle pill peddlers. But the truth is, we all lie—*especially* to ourselves. At some point, we've all told ourselves, *I'm going to turn off my phone an hour before bedtime, I'll stop after I watch just* one *more video*, or *It's fine. I'm fine. Everything is fine.*

Avoiding, minimizing, or denying painful truths is a common experience. As author Gertrude Atherton put it, "The human mind has an infinite capacity for self-deception."[*] Although self-deception is a shared human experience, it is important to remember the following two things:

⌖ The absence of honesty creates the presence of pathology.[†]

⌖ An uncomfortable truth is preferable to a shiny lie.[‡]

❁ Quiz: Liar, Liar, Pants on Fire

Instructions: Put a check mark next to any of the following untruths you've ever thought or said. Give yourself one point for each check mark.

---

[*] "The chief problem facing intentional models of self-deception is the dynamic paradox, namely, that it seems impossible to form an intention to get oneself to believe what one currently disbelieves or believes is false." ("Self-Deception," *Stanford Encyclopedia of Philosophy*, March 13, 2023, https://plato.stanford.edu/entries/self-deception.) In plain language: there seems always to be a part of ourselves that knows what we know and another part that tries to keep us away from what we know.

[†] *Pathology* (or *psychopathology*) is the clinical way of saying "the behavior is bad."

[‡] This principle is mostly true. If you are caring for someone with dementia or trying to get someone in active psychosis to safety, truth can create unsafe conditions. Although it certainly should not be the default choice, there are times when lying is 100 percent appropriate.

	I'm good.	
	Yes, I'm happy to help.	
	Nothing is wrong.	
	Sorry! I haven't checked my phone all day.	
	I don't have time.	
	I'm only going to have one glass of wine.	
	I'll get to the gym tomorrow.	
	I can't . . . I have a headache.	
	I'm too old/it's too late.	
	It wasn't *that* bad.	
	I always love being a parent.	
	I always love being a partner.	
	I'm better off staying where I am.	
	I'm on my way.	
	It must have gone into my spam folder.	
	My phone died.	
	We should get together.	
	Yes, I can _____.	
	No, I can't _____.	
	I'll be happy when I have _____.	

If you scored zero to five: You are a wise caterpillar. Please teach us all your ways.

If you scored six to ten: You likely have set a few boundaries and prioritized yourself. Well done.

If you scored eleven to fifteen: You're probably feeling overwhelmed, stressed, and burned out.

If you scored sixteen to twenty: Welcome to the Liars Club. We have jackets.

Why Do We Lie?

Neuroscientist Amishi Jha explains, "There is far more information in our environment (and in our own minds!) than the brain can fully process. Without a way to filter, the relentless sensory input would leave us overloaded, incapable of functioning effectively."* One of your brain's most useful filtration systems is *bias*. Bias, which simply means a bend or tendency toward or against something, is used (to a degree) by all humans. Even the most intelligent and rational person is biased. Why? Author Buster Benson put it best: "Because thinking is hard."

Your brain diligently works on your behalf every second of every day—and many of its activities are automatic. Rather than shaming yourself for having biases, bringing cognitive biases (or thought filters) to conscious awareness prevents you from being unconsciously driven by them. Or as founder of the School of Thought International Jesse Richardson put it in his TEDx Talk, "Never trust a brain. Especially your own."

❧ Fact or Opinion?

Instructions: Fill in the chart below with a list of any troubling, looping, or uncomfortable thoughts and then check whether they're fact or opinion. I've added several examples to get you started. Notice if there are any thoughts you are quick to label as facts when they're actually opinions.

Thought	Fact	Opinion
I am lazy.		X
I am crazy.		X
I am a bad person.		X
It is difficult homeschooling children and caring for aging parents.	X	

---

* Amishi Jha, "The Brain Science of Attention and Overwhelm," Mindful, November 5, 2020, https://www.mindful.org/youre-overwhelmed-and-its-not-your-fault.

Thought	Fact	Opinion

💭 Put Your Thoughts on Trial

Instructions: Fill in the blanks in the following chart. Read the example to get started.

Troubling Thought	Evidence to Support This Thought	Evidence to Disprove This Thought	What Is a Consequence of Believing the Troubling Thought?	What Is a Better Way of Framing the Troubling Thought?
I am a terrible person.	I yelled at my kids, I didn't take the dog out this morning, and I haven't showered in a week.	I pack the kids' lunches every day, most people would say I'm a decent person, and I'm always the first one to volunteer when someone needs help moving.	When I believe I'm a terrible person, I feel depressed and anxious. When I'm depressed and anxious, I tend to numb out and distract myself with food and doomscrolling.	I make mistakes more than I wish I would, but there is evidence to support that I'm not 100 percent a bad person.

Troubling Thought	Evidence to Support This Thought	Evidence to Disprove This Thought	What Is a Consequence of Believing the Troubling Thought?	What Is a Better Way of Framing the Troubling Thought?

 **Check-In**

Instructions: Either think about the following questions or write about them in your journal.

- ▸ How did you feel about doing these thought exercises?
- ▸ Did you notice any resistance to doing these exercises?
- ▸ How are you doing with your daily practice?

Observation: One takeaway from this work is:

_____

Recommendation: Something I can do with this information is:

_____

Information Overload

It can be tough to know what to believe these days. A scroll through any news site can have you convinced we're all going to die of monkeypox or a zombie apocalypse. My friend David McRaney, author of *You Are Not So Smart* (and several other must-read books), writes: "If you see lots of shark attacks in the news, you think, 'Gosh, sharks are out of control.' What you should think is, 'Gosh, the news loves to cover shark attacks.'" He also reminds us of this important life lesson: "THE MISCONCEPTION: You are a rational, logical being who sees the world as it really is. THE TRUTH: You are as deluded as the rest of us, but that's OK, it keeps you sane."

If you're feeling nervous because you're starting to recognize how often your brain runs the show without your input, it is super important to note two things:

⚷ Radical honesty + self-compassion = *change*

⚷ Radical honesty + self-blame = *stuck*

Self-Compassion—Not Just Butterflies and Rainbows

Getting honest about dishonesty is squirmy work, but shame is an unwelcome visitor in the process. Shaming yourself is not only unnecessary, it is 100 percent unhelpful. Remind yourself, gently and often, that if beating yourself up for your thoughts and behaviors worked, it would have worked by now. Self-compassion is not the same as self-justification. You can take accountability for your behavior while simultaneously extending compassion to yourself.

Still not convinced?

If you think self-compassion is saccharine, mushy, and toothless, there's science to back it up. An article from Stanford Medicine says: "Though the term 'self-compassion' may sound like self-indulgence or may feel like a weakness, it is actually the secret to resilience, strength in the face of failure, the ability to learn from mistakes and to bounce back with greater enthusiasm."* Countless evidenced-based studies cite the many benefits of self-compassion, including increased resilience, productivity, and decreased stress.

1. You are stressed

2. You beat yourself up

3. Your brain releases STRESS HORMONES

4. You make bad choices

VERSUS

1. You are stressed

2. You say kind things to yourself

3. Your brain does NOT flood you with stress hormones

4. You make good choices

---

* Emma Seppälä, PhD, "The Scientific Benefits of Self-Compassion," Stanford Medicine, The Center for Compassion and Altruism Research and Education, May 8, 2014, http://ccare.stanford.edu/uncategorized/the-scientific-benefits-of-self-compassion-infographic.

As my dear friend Vanessa Cornell, founder of the global women's collective NUSHU, says, "The number one indicator of someone's capacity for personal development is their willingness to be deeply honest with themselves—*plus* their ability to practice radical self-compassion in the face of that honesty." Seeking to be "good" is an exercise in futility. We carry within us the entire spectrum of human potential—the potential for greatness and the potential for evil. The only way to be a "good" person all the time is to split your psyche, to lie to yourself, or to lie to others. Seeking to be whole, honest, and connected requires curiosity and willingness—no exorcisms or self-shame required.

♥ **Self-Compassion Journal Prompts**

Instructions: Read through the following prompts and then write on one, two, or all of them. If you're not sure where to start, try choosing one that feels easy and then choose one that feels uncomfortable.

Journal Prompt 1: Befriending Yourself

Think of something you constantly beat yourself up for doing or thinking. It can be a bad habit, an unhealthy relationship pattern, or a task you've been avoiding. Write a letter to yourself as if you were talking to a friend. How would you encourage them? Would you be critical and harsh or curious and kind? Would you be understanding and offer support, or would you use abusive name-calling and threatening language?

Journal Prompt 2: What's Bothering You?

All the behaviors, habits, and patterns we don't like about ourselves usually are there to help us avoid pain. What about your life is causing you pain, discomfort, or fear? Allow yourself to be honest about what is upsetting you right now. Don't hold back how you *really* feel about your boss, your spouse, or your siblings. If parts of you are worried that putting this to paper will cause harm to someone, you can burn it when you're done. If parts of you feel guilty for putting your thoughts on paper, remind them that feeling wholeness (and happiness) requires honesty.

Journal Prompt 3: What Would They Say About You?

Consider what your closest friend would say about you if asked. Write down what you think they would say, and go into as much detail as possible about your strengths, gifts, and talents. Remind yourself that this exercise is for your eyes only, so don't be afraid to brag. If you are completely blank and have zero clue where to start, you can call a friend and ask for help with this exercise.

Journal Prompt 4: Letter to Your Younger Self

Write a letter to your younger self from your current self. What have you learned that you wish they would have known? How would you encourage them? What do they need to hear most? If you have children, write this letter as compassionately as a loving parent. If you have nieces or nephews, write this letter as their favorite aunt or uncle. If you are more of an animal person than a people person, write this letter with the same love and care you give your pets.

Journal Prompt 5: Letter from Your Future Self

Write a letter to your current self from your future self. What do you need to hear most right now? What life do you hope this future version of yourself is living? What wisdom or guidance would future you want to share with current you?

Journal Prompt 6: Stronger Than You Think

Think of a moment in the past year when you surprised yourself with your capacity. It could be the way you showed up for a friend, the way you navigated someone through a medical or relationship crisis, or the way you managed to keep the kids fed and clothed even though you felt like staying in bed all day.

Journal Prompt 7: Trimming the Fat

Think of all the obligations and things on your plate each week. Are there any areas where you could cut corners without causing harm? This could be something like bringing store-bought cupcakes to the class party instead of making them from scratch or allowing yourself to use some of that time off you *know* you have available.

 **Check-In**

Instructions: Either think about the following questions or write about them in your journal.

- How was your experience doing these journal prompts and reading this material so far?
- Did you notice any resistance?
- Did you hear parts of yourself going, "Well, yes, *but . . .*" anytime you tried to be nice to yourself?
- Do you feel the need to prove why you don't deserve or need self-compassion?
- How are you doing with your daily practice?

Observation: One takeaway from this work is:

_____

Recommendation: Something I can do with this information is:

_____

When you build your self-awareness and self-compassion muscles, you are less likely to give your time, energy, and money to things that do not serve your life. As decluttering expert Marie Kondo teaches in *The Life-Changing Magic of Tidying Up*, "To truly cherish the things that are important to you, you must first discard those that have outlived their purpose." This philosophy is as relevant to self-care routines as it is to possessions. Remind yourself, gently and often, that the work of decluttering your wellness practices is well worth the effort. The next section shows you how.

The Dark Side of Light Work

All practices and products can cause problems, but you'd never know it from the "gurus" who preach the gospel of trends like teatoxing* or jade eggs.† The phrase *cult favorite* refers to "the devoted fanatics that spring up around particular products, regardless of their price point and availability."‡ Although this term usually is associated with beauty products and household items, cult favorite wellness practices regularly spring up on social media platforms, too. Some of these practices, for some people, in some cases, work beautifully. But they do not work for every person in every situation. If you've ever felt confused or frustrated by the ineffectiveness of even your best efforts, you may find the next challenge helpful.

👣 The Shadow Side of Self-Care

Instructions: Read through each of the following cult favorite practices, and do the suggested prescription. (Or create one of your own, or decide to stop doing the practice altogether.) You can do one or as many of these as you want.

---

*Detox teas often contain laxatives, which is a dangerous way to drop pounds. A *Consumer Reports* article notes, "That lower number won't stay down . . . if you weigh yourself after you have diarrhea because of a laxative you're going to weigh less . . . but now you're relatively dehydrated. As soon as you drink enough to be properly hydrated, your weight will be identical to what it was." (Amy O'Connor, "Should You Try a Teatox?" *Consumer Reports*, May 15, 2018, https://www.consumerreports.org.)

†The "jade egg" trend involves shoving an egg-shaped rock inside the vagina to build pelvic floor strength. Some swear by this, but there is no medical evidence to prove the efficacy of jade eggs. Blogger Madison Higgins Hwang said it best: "There are better, cheaper, and safer ways to strengthen your pelvic floor. None of which include a vagina omelette." (Madison Higgins Hwang, "The 10 Wildest Wellness Trends from the Past Decade," *Darcy Magazine*, December 27, 2021, https://darcymagazine.com/wellness-trends/.)

‡Zan Romanoff, "What 'Cult' Means When It Comes to Beauty," Racked, March 9, 2018, https://www.racked.com/2018/3/9/17064236/cult-beauty-products.

1. The Practice: Forgiveness

The promise: Forgiveness will heal you and set you free.

The problem: Forgiveness is a beautiful spiritual ideal, but it is *not* required to create new neural pathways. Forgiveness requires the cognitive capacity to make rational choices, and you can make rational choices only when your brain is no longer stuck in survival mode.

The prescription: Remind yourself that although forgiveness is often a by-product of healing, it is *not* mandatory. You do *not* need to forgive to heal. Think of one person you are struggling to forgive. Decide (at least for now) to allow yourself *not* to forgive them. Use that energy on one self-care activity that will help you feel nurtured.

2. The Practice: Breathwork

The promise: Breathwork will hack your vagus nerve, heal your anxiety, calm your body, and improve your health.

The problem: Forcing breath can re-traumatize your system. If you have medical trauma, being told to "take a deep breath" can be triggering. For sexual or assault trauma survivors, forcing *anything* into our bodies, including breath, can create a panic response.

The prescription: Remind yourself that breathwork is a wonderful option in *some* cases, for *some* people. If it doesn't work for you, that is not your fault. In my practice I often recommend breathwork to clients but do not use it in my personal recovery process.* If you are in a class or session in which you are told how to breathe, ignore the direction and breathe however you want.

---

*There are incredible trauma-informed breathwork practitioners who are aware of the limits of and potential problems with breathwork. If you want to try breathwork, ask your practitioner if you can modify any practices that feel uncomfortable or unsafe for you.

3. The Practice: Psychotherapy

The promise: Doing therapy will heal your trauma and decrease your anxiety and depression.

The problem: Not all therapists are trauma informed, not all therapists have neuroscience training, not all therapists are skillful, and not all therapists are ethical.

The prescription: Remind yourself that the goal of therapy isn't to change yourself—it's to know yourself. A therapist is there to guide, not advise or dictate. A safe therapist should help you find *your* truth, not try to sell you on *theirs*.

4. The Practice: Meditation

The promise: Meditation is the panacea for all life's problems. Meditation will slow your racing thoughts, give you inner peace, reduce your anxiety, and heal your heart.

The problem: Meditation can feel disorienting at best and terrifying at worst. "Quieting your mind" and "noticing your thoughts" is not always a helpful practice, nor is it always a safe practice.

The prescription: Instead of trying to "go inside" and notice your thoughts and feelings, try meditating *outward* by focusing your attention on what you can see, hear, smell, touch, and taste.

5. The Practice: Cold Water Immersion

The promise: Cold plunges will heal your body, focus your mind, give you energy, regulate your nervous system, manage your stress, and improve your sleep.

The problem: The science of cold plunges is encouraging, but for some people, in some cases, the jolt* from a cold plunge can create anxiety and trauma responses.

---

*The placebo effect is also a factor. A *New York Times* article noted, "Not only are swimmers immersing themselves in frigid water, but they are also often exercising, socializing, spending time outdoors and taking on a

Potential physiological consequences include arrhythmia, heart attack, hyperventilation, or hypothermia.

The prescription: If a full-body immersion doesn't work for you, you can modify the practice by putting your face or your feet into a bowl of ice water. You also can try holding ice cubes and notice them melting in your hands. Or you can abstain from cold water techniques completely.

6. The Practice: Accountability Partners

The promise: Accountability partners (or groups) will prevent procrastination, increase motivation, help you achieve goals, and improve performance.

The problem: There is a fine line between accountability and control. When you constantly rely on other people to "make" you stick to your plans, you create a parent/child dynamic and abdicate sovereignty over your life. Accountability partners who are punitive or controlling create emotionally abusive dynamics, and groups that prioritize accountability over authenticity are breeding grounds for dishonesty.

The prescription: If you choose to use an accountability group or partner, make it clear to them, and to yourself, that their job is to support and encourage, *not* to be your commanding officer or behavioral manager.

7. The Practice: Sharing Your Story

The promise: Sharing your story will give you a sense of belonging and connection. It will help you heal your trauma.

The problem: Sharing your story in chronological order, even with safe people, can activate or re-traumatize your nervous system. Sometimes the practice of sharing

---

challenge—all of which may boost mental health." (Tyler Comrie, "Cold Water Plunges Are Trendy. Can They Really Reduce Anxiety and Depression?" *The New York Times*, February 21, 2022, https://www.nytimes.com /2022/02/20/well/mind/cold-water-plunge-mental-health.html.)

morphs into *traumaholism*—the compulsion to tell our trauma stories over and over. When we compulsively share our stories, we are usually dissociated while sharing. (This is when you can describe a traumatic event without feeling anything.) Dissociated sharing is seldom helpful.

The prescription: If you are going to share your story, try to only share it with safe people. If you choose to share your story repeatedly, try to tell it in nonchronological order, and refrain from going into detail.

8. **The Practice: Exercise**

The promise: Exercise will elevate your mood, increase your brainpower, lower your stress, and increase your energy.

The problem: Overexercise is physically and emotionally harmful. Prioritizing hard-core exercising over much-needed rest can lead to burnout and injury. Overexercise can lead to a sluggish metabolism, eating disorders, amenorrhea,[*] and fatigue.

The prescription: Be sure you are eating enough food to support the work you're asking your body to do. Remind yourself that rest is a biological imperative, not a sign of weakness. Avoid training the same muscle groups back-to-back on consecutive days. If possible, seek out support if you find that you experience anxiety or panic at the thought of missing a workout.

9. **The Practice: "Clean" Eating**

The promise: "Clean" eating will improve your health, increase your energy, boost your metabolism, improve your sex life, relieve chronic pain, and free you from cravings.

---

[*] Amenorrhea is the absence of a menstrual period. Exercise-induced amenorrhea is a thing. At the peak of my eating disorder, I was so underweight that I lost my period for years.

The problem: "Clean" is a misnomer when it comes to food. The only "dirty" food is food that has fallen onto the floor. When we refer to foods as "clean" and "dirty," we ignore the reality of food insecurity and create a hierarchy of superiority. The obsession with only consuming "clean" food is a lesser known but still devastating eating disorder called orthorexia.*

The prescription: Remove the labels of "clean and dirty" and "good and bad" from your food. Focus on how the food makes you feel. Remember that emotional eating is not always harmful. Food is enjoyable, and you're allowed to eat for enjoyment. A mindful approach to eating is preferable to a rigid approach. When a "clean diet" creates anxiety, fear, and avoidance, it becomes a stress enhancer rather than a stress reliever.

10. The Practice: Positive Thinking

The promise: Positive thinking will improve your relationships, prevent intrusive thoughts, reduce depression, improve self-esteem, and boost your immune system.

The problem: When positive thinking ignores or minimizes the reality of discomfort and pain, it morphs into self-inflicted gaslighting.

The prescription: Instead of focusing on *positive* thinking, try *realistic* thinking. Ask yourself, *How true is this thought?* and *Is the story I'm telling myself the* full *story?*

That last one, positive thinking, is perhaps the most common—and problematic—practice in the modern wellness world. Cheeky decor, T-shirts, and coffee mugs proclaim, *Good Vibes Always, Positive Mind = Positive Life*, and *Keep Calm and Poop Rainbows*. (Yes, that last one is real.) But remember a key point from earlier in this part: an uncomfortable truth is preferable to a shiny lie.

Positive thinking is not *realistic* thinking. It is rare that situations are ever completely

---

* I had a personal bout of orthorexia when I was terrified to eat any food that had more than five ingredients. I obsessively read labels, refused to participate in social activities, and experienced panic episodes if I was forced to consume anything with ingredients I couldn't pronounce.

positive or completely negative.* In addition to not being realistic, positive thinking denies you the gifts that come with challenges. Author Mark Manson notes: "Everything worthwhile in life is won through surmounting the associated negative experience. Any attempt to escape the negative, to avoid it or quash it or silence it, only backfires. The avoidance of suffering is a form of suffering. The avoidance of struggle is a struggle. The denial of failure is a failure. Hiding what is shameful is itself a form of shame."

⊶O Positive thinking ignores the reality of pain. Negative thinking ignores the reality of resources. We need both.

The best hack I've ever seen for integrating positive and negative thinking comes from a surprising place—the comedy improv world. The next section gives you a time-honored way to reframe your thoughts so you can avoid the cognitive distortion rabbit hole.

Improv Rules for Life

In the comedy improv world, one of the most known techniques is called the "Yes, and . . ." rule. This rule helps prevent actors from getting stuck in their scenes. It also allows stories to develop in entertaining and unexpected ways. The "Yes, and . . ." rule says, "If someone presents a reality to you, however ridiculous it may seem, you accept it and build upon it, sometimes redirecting toward something you're more comfortable with, and sometimes continuing down the rabbit hole they've created. More simply, you don't tell someone no. You respond 'Yes, and . . .'"†

In Tina Fey's hilarious memoir, *Bossy Pants*, she writes: "The first rule of improv is

---

*Certain *events* like abuse, racism, oppression, etc. are always negative. But if the story you're telling yourself about the event is, *I am a terrible person because this terrible thing happened to me and no one will ever love me,* then it is the *story's* negativity you are challenging, not the event itself.

†Sam Killermann, "Mastering the 'Yes, and . . .' Rule," Safe Zone Project, August 2, 2018, https://thesafezone project.com/yes-and-rule.

AGREE. Always agree and SAY YES . . . the second rule of improvisation is not only to say yes, but YES, AND. You are supposed to agree and then add something of your own." The power of the "Yes, and . . ." rule is not limited to the arts. It also is a hacksaw for amputating shame. When you argue with yourself and get locked into binary thinking, wholeness is inaccessible, shame is inevitable, and the shadow gains strength. Carl Jung talked about the necessity to hold multiple realities. He wrote: "On the individual level, we each must 'stand the tension of opposites' in ourselves. Each of us is being asked by the realities of our world to take up the task of integrating the shadow, and it is not an easy task, for it requires engagement with the unconscious."* A user-friendly method for holding the "tension of opposites" inside yourself is dialectical behavioral therapy (DBT).†

DBT clears the Bandersnatch‡ and bramble that bestrew life's messy middle paths. The tools focus on four areas:

1. Mindfulness (keeping your head where your feet are)
2. Emotional regulation (putting out your brain when it's on fire)
3. Distress tolerance (making uncomfortable body sensations bearable)
4. Interpersonal effectiveness (boundary setting and communication skills)

At the apex of my breakdown, this type of therapy was a game changer, and I often incorporate DBT techniques into my professional practice.§ When I am working with clients, one of the fastest ways to ease the pressure of perfection is to create space for multiple

---

* "Jung's Challenge to Us: Holding the Tension of the Opposites," Jungian Center for the Spiritual Sciences, https://jungiancenter.org/jungs-challenge-to-us-holding-the-tension-of-the-opposites.

† DBT was created by Marsha Linehan and is often recommended for the treatment of what the mental health world calls borderline personality disorder. That diagnosis is BS, but DBT therapy is solid, and I spent a year of my personal recovery participating in it.

‡ This made-up word comes from the poem "Jabberwocky." Lewis Carroll invented nonsensical words, and he originated the phrase *portmanteau word*. "A *portmanteau word* is a word that has been made by blending two words together. Think *brunch* (*breakfast* and *lunch*), *smog* (*smoke* and *fog*) and *spork* (*spoon* and *fork*)." ("The Frabjous Words Invented by Lewis Carroll," Dictionary.com, June 26, 2020, https://www.dictionary.com/e/words-invented-by-lewis-carroll.)

§ Important to note: DBT is a fantastic tool for developing coping skills, but it is not a trauma healing approach. DBT helps people *cope* with trauma; it does not help metabolize or heal trauma. DBT is often necessary before attempting a trauma healing approach, especially if there are behavioral challenges like active addiction or suicidal ideation.

truths like "I love my kids" *and* "Sometimes I don't like being a parent." F. Scott Fitzgerald wrote: "The test of a first-rate intelligence is the ability to hold two opposed ideas in mind at the same time and still retain the ability to function." The following challenges help you create the internal space you need to hold two opposing ideas at the same time.

Make a "Yes, and . . ." List

Instructions: In the first column in the following chart, make a list of all the things about yourself that you feel ashamed for thinking or doing. Then, in the "Yes, and . . ." column, add another piece of information that is also true. I've added examples to get you started.

Sometimes I Feel Bad That I . . .	Yes, and . . .
Really don't like my parents.	I really love my parents.
Judge my friends.	When my friends are sick, I'm usually the first one to bring them soup.
Don't care about what's going on in the world.	I want to be helpful to my community and make a difference in the world.

Make a "Gratitude, and . . ." List

Instructions: Gratitude is a wonderful practice. Ruminating about problems without accessing gratitude creates entitlement. But gratitude that doesn't acknowledge the reality of pain creates a lacquered veneer under which lies decay. We need to acknowledge gratitude and pain. On the chart below, list things you are grateful for and then list something that is also true in the right column.

I'm Grateful for . . .	Yes, and . . .
Having running water and electricity.	Sometimes I feel frustrated that there's too much month at the end of my money.
My family.	Sometimes my family really upsets me.

☕ Check-In

Instructions: Either think about the following questions or write about them in your journal.

- ▸ How did it feel to create your "Yes, and . . ." list?
- ▸ How did it feel to create your "Gratitude, and . . ." list?
- ▸ Did you find yourself wanting to return to all-or-nothing thinking?
- ▸ Notice your body as you reread your statements. Do you feel more expansive? More constricted? Dissociated?
- ▸ What surprised you about this exercise?
- ▸ How are you doing with your daily practice?

Observation: One takeaway from this work is:

_____

Recommendation: Something I can do with this information is:

_____

"How Do You Feel?"

One of my pet-peeve questions is "How do you feel?" Many people, including me, often struggle to understand our feelings. As a therapist, I try to avoid asking the "How do you feel?" question altogether. Feelings are confusing, they're often fickle, and feelings literacy is *not* the cultural norm—I certainly didn't grow up understanding how to decode my feelings (and if you're reading this, I suspect you didn't either). The next section is a crash course on understanding and working with feelings. If you're tempted to skip this section because feelings are gross (I hear you), remember that anytime you gloss over your feelings to get to a desired outcome, the result is a shiny lie.

What does the shiny lie look like?

The shiny lie looks like achieving your fitness goals but still feeling ashamed of your body. The shiny lie looks like sitting in the C-suite but still believing you're an imposter. The shiny lie looks like a perfectly curated family photo, but behind closed doors there's a nightly war over bedtime. The shiny lie also looks like having most of your comfort and security needs met but continuing to experience emptiness and unhappiness. If you want to feel better, feelings work is nonnegotiable. I don't particularly enjoy distressing feelings, but happiness requires wholeness, and wholeness is impossible if you ignore your feelings.

⚷ Feeling your feelings can be a bummer, but the alternative is worse. Promise.

The next four exercises likely are going to be uncomfortable because they're intended to unearth "negative" shadow qualities like anger, jealousy, fear, and guilt. Each shadow quality is a trail marker; for example, jealousy directs you toward desire, and anger directs you toward injustice. To be happy, you need to be whole, and wholeness means accepting positive and negative qualities about the world—and about yourself.

Pace yourself, and do what you're able. Refuse to shame yourself along the way. Suzy Kassem wrote: "Nobody is purely good or purely evil. Most of us are in-between. There are moths that explore the day and butterflies that play at night. Polarity is an integral part of nature—human or not human." Take breaks, skip the material if necessary, and approach the actions *only* when you are in a safe place and are rested, fed, and emotionally regulated. If you have a therapist or coach, you may find it helpful to bring these challenges into your sessions.

Off we go . . .

❧ 1. Shadow Inventory

Instructions: Fill in the blanks. Don't worry about analyzing the origin of your answers or trying to figure out "what to do" with them right now. The point of this task is to excavate some of the less socially acceptable feelings hiding in your shadow, not to shame yourself for what you find. Warning: This task can bring up strong feelings. Remember that shadow work can be unpleasant but should never feel unsafe. Take a break if you start to feel overwhelmed.

I experience guilt when _____.

I experience sadness when _____.

I experience fear when _____.

If I could get away with it, I'd _____.

I experience embarrassment when _____.

The thing that bothers me the most about myself is _____.

One thing I'm super resentful about is _____.

I would be mortified if anyone knew that I _____.

Something I'm ashamed to admit about myself is that I _____.

Something I'm upset about but haven't told anyone is _____.

Something I'm sad about but haven't told anyone is _____.

Something I'm worried about but haven't told anyone is _____.

The thing I think most people misunderstand about me is _____.

The thing I wish people would understand about me is _____.

Something I do that causes me to experience shame is _____.

My biggest secret is _____.

♥ 2. Fear and Rejection Inventory

Instructions: Fill in the blanks. Don't judge. Notice with curiosity.

I'm afraid if I say _____, people will think _____.

I'm afraid if I do _____, people will think _____.

I'm afraid if I want _____, people will think _____.

I'm afraid if I let myself admit _____, _____ will happen.

I'm afraid most people are _____.

My greatest fear about my family is _____.

My greatest fear about my life is _____.

My greatest fear about myself is _____.

If I knew I wasn't going to be rejected, I would _____.

✿ 3. Getting to Know Your Anger

Anger that is allowed to roam freely is dangerous and harmful to other people. But refusing to acknowledge anger is dangerous and harmful to yourself. "Anger is an integral part of our fight-or-flight mechanism. It had a survival necessity in the past and has some positive value in the present, too. The motivation and action that is powered by anger can move us toward reaching our goals. It pushes us to fix the wrongs we see in the world and make it right."* The goal is not to *avoid* anger, but to skillfully work *through* it.

Instructions: Think of someone for whom you currently feel anger. Notice the anger in your body. Imagine it has a shape, color, and texture. Put your hand on the area of your body where you feel the anger. What do you think your anger would want you to understand? You can think about this question or write down your thoughts in your journal.

♥ 4. Befriending the Green-Eyed Monster of Jealousy†

No one, including me, likes to admit they feel jealous. It's not a good look on anyone, and our bias against jealousy makes a lot of sense. Jealousy eats away at relationships, creates tension and resentment, and squeezes out all sense of playfulness or creativity. But it's not skillful humaning to deny its presence, and people who refuse to work through jealousy eventually wind up bitter and friendless.‡ There's no need to fear jealousy. The quality itself isn't the problem; the problem is *unsupervised* jealousy. Jealousy that is cared for with curiosity unlocks clarity.

⌐O Jealousy cues are *clues*. If you're feeling jealous, there's an authentic desire to be discovered.

Instructions: Fill in the chart with real or fictional people. These can be people you know or people you've never met. If you're not sure who sparks jealousy, look through your social media feed and pay attention to your reactions.

---

* Moshe Ratson, MBA, MS, LMFT, "The Value of Anger: 16 Reasons It's Good to Get Angry," GoodTherapy, March 13, 2017, https://www.goodtherapy.org/blog/value-of-anger-16-reasons-its-good-to-get-angry-0313175.

† Fun fact: "Some believe the color green has been associated with jealousy dating back to the ancient Greeks. They believed jealousy occurred as a result of the overproduction of bile, which turned human skin slightly green." ("Why Do People Describe Envy and Jealousy in Shades of Green?" Sharecare, https://www.sharecare.com/health /feelings-emotions-relationships/why-describe-jealousy-shades-green.)

‡ In Tim Burton's adaptation of *Alice in Wonderland*, jealousy is the origin of the sociopathic narcissism displayed by the Red Queen (who is fond of decapitating people).

If you get stuck on what to put in the action column, know that it doesn't have to be big. There is almost always a step you can take. You may not be able to take a month-long vacation, but perhaps you could plan a day trip. You may not have the ability right now to buy your dream home, but you can create a Pinterest board with furniture you'd like to put in it one day.

I'm Jealous of . . .	What About Them Causes Me to Feel Jealous?	What Desire Do I Think My Jealousy Is Trying to Tell Me?	What's One Tiny Action I Can Take in the Direction of This Desire?
I'm jealous of the travel blogger who always pops up on my feed.	I'm jealous that they get to travel and go on so many vacations.	My jealousy is telling me that I have a desire to travel and take time off work.	I can use one of my PTO days to take a day trip in the next month. And I can start looking at flights and Airbnb options for a longer trip in the future.

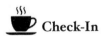 **Check-In**

Instructions: Either think about the following questions or write about them in your journal.

- How did you do with the four actions?
- Which of the actions were the hardest? Which was easiest?
- What surprised you about your responses?
- How are you doing with your daily practice?

Observation: One takeaway from this work is:

_____

Recommendation: Something I can do with this information is:

_____

Feelings and Thoughts and Emotions . . . Oh My

We often interchange words like *feelings*, *thoughts*, and *emotions*, but it is important to recognize their differences. Why? It's nearly impossible to successfully manage your feelings if they are mixed into the same pile as your thoughts and emotions. For example:

- "I really feel like you don't understand me" is not a feeling; it's a thought.
- "I really feel like nothing will ever work out for me" is also a thought.
- "I feel like no matter how hard I try, I can't seem to get moving"—this, too, is a thought and not a feeling.

Hmm.

If all the previous statements are thoughts, then what are feelings? Simply put, feelings are *body sensations*. When you understand that feelings are first physiological—not mental, moral, or metaphysical—they become less scary, and you won't have to work as hard to avoid them. It's normal to assume that all uncomfortable feelings are *bad* and all comfortable feelings are *good*. But this assumption is inaccurate and a sign that the trickster brain is in action. Happiness often feels like taking a bath in warm honey, but so does an opiate high. Fear often feels like muscle tension, fast breathing, and a racing heart, but so does good sex.

Feelings, Thoughts, and Emotions: What's the Difference?

▸ **Feelings:** Body sensations (tight, buzzy, warm, loose, clenched, tingly, cold, tense)

▸ **Thoughts:** Mental constructs (ideas, opinions, stories, images, dreams, decisions)

▸ **Emotions:** Body sensations with a thought or story attached (fear, anger, shame, love, sadness)

It's totally fine to intermix words when things are running smoothly. But if you're stressed, anxious, depressed, or burned out, that's your cue to slow down and disentangle the knot of feelings, thoughts, or emotions. *Feelings* do not have any meaning or story attached to them; they are physiological body sensations. *Thoughts* are in your head and may or may not include a body sensation. *Emotions* are the result of adding a *thought* or a *story* to your body sensations. For example:

Scenario 1: You notice the body sensations (feelings) of sweaty palms, a dry mouth, and tension in your stomach. If the story (thought) you attach to these body sensations is that you're about to go on a date, you'd label the emotion *excitement*.

Scenario 2: You notice the same body sensations (feelings) of sweaty palms, a dry mouth, and tension in your stomach. But this time, if the story (thought) you attach to these body sensations is that you just got called into your boss's office, you'd label the emotion *fear*.

🔑 **The same set of body sensations (feelings) can create completely different emotions depending on the story (thought).**

Attaching meaning to body sensations is often automatic and unconscious, but you *can* train your brain to not automatically believe its own stories. How? The next exercise is adapted from a therapy approach called rational emotive behavior therapy, or REBT.* (Yes, that name is an epic snoozefest.) Although it sounds a bit pompous and prancy, REBT is useful because when you tell yourself inaccurate stories about your body sensations, you accidentally add unnecessary stress to your system. REBT is like the Container Store—it offers all the bins, labels, and organizational contraptions you could ever need to tidy up your mind closet. You can't change your past, but you *can* rearrange how it's stored so your stuff doesn't fall on your head every time you open the door.

⚿ A big, giant disclaimer:

REBT or CBT exercises are *not* recommended if the story is related to abuse, natural disaster, war, assault, or any traumatizing event. The goal is to challenge potentially faulty assumptions, not to gaslight yourself out of being appropriately upset or angry relative to the situation.

💭 Challenge Your Thoughts to Change Your Emotions

Instructions: Think of stressful events that cause you to experience the emotions of shame, anger, guilt, or fear and then complete the chart on the next page. I've added some examples to get you started.

Disclaimer: Be careful not to slip into wishful thinking while attempting this exercise. If someone causes you harm or if you were in a traumatic situation, don't use those examples in this exercise. Telling yourself, "Well, they didn't mean it" or "I suppose everything happens for a reason" is *not* helpful.

---

* "Albert Ellis (1913–2007) was one of the most influential psychotherapists in history. He created rational emotive behavior therapy (REBT), which was part of psychotherapy's cognitive revolution and served as a foundation for cognitive-behavioral therapy." (Cynthia Vinney, "Biography of Albert Ellis, Creator of Rational Emotive Behavior Therapy," ThoughtCo. August 31, 2019, https://www.thoughtco.com/albert-ellis-4768692.)

Triggering Event	Thoughts About the Event	Resulting Emotion	Resulting Behavior	Is There Another Thought That Also Could Be True?	New Emotion and Behavior
Someone cut me off on the highway.	That jerk did that to me on purpose.	Rage	Going home and yelling at the dog.	Maybe that person didn't see me, or maybe they were in a rush to get to a sick relative.	Annoyed, but able to continue driving without incident.
My friend didn't text me back.	They hate me. Everyone hates me. I'm a terrible person.	Shame	Checking their social media to see what they're doing and then spending the next four hours doomscrolling.	Maybe they are busy and didn't see my text.	Go about my day and remind myself they'll get back to me when they're able.

The previous exercise helps you slow down and categorize the juggernaut of events, stories, or emotions that create much of the chaos in life. If you're able to change or re-frame the story (which is *sometimes* possible but not always), you can shift your emotions. A quick hack when you are triggered by an event is to focus on your *story*, not the event or emotions. A helpful mnemonic when you're feeling uncomfortable is to remember the phrase, "This Stinks" (trigger + story).

🔑 **Assuming the trigger isn't abuse, war, racism, social inequality, etc., it can be helpful to ask, "Is it possible there's another story besides the one I'm telling myself?"**

There are instances when the stories that accompany events are immutable. For example, oppression is universally horrific, abuse is never your fault, and eating Tide Pods is always bad.* Sometimes, the stories we tell ourselves are just flat-out inaccurate. But there are other instances when the stories we make up about other people are unpleasant truths about *ourselves* we want to avoid. This is a type of cognitive bias (and classic Freudian defense mechanism) called *projection*.†

Projection: If You Spot It, You Got It‡

Projection is when we are unconscious of our own thoughts/feelings/biases and attribute them to another person. As problematic as much of Freud's work is, he was spot-on in naming projection as the shadow quality behind many relational conflicts.

Sometimes when we think, *That person must hate me*, it's because we don't like *them*. Sometimes we judge other people for being too thin, fat, loud, quiet, rich, or poor because we feel insecure about our *own* bodies, personalities, or finances. The next two tasks are designed to help you identify and withdraw your projections.

---

* The "Tide Pod challenge" was a 2018 TikTok trend that encouraged users to ingest laundry pods. WTF?

† Fun party fact: Sigmund Freud "borrowed the word *projection* from neurology, where it referred to the inherent capacity of neurons to transmit stimuli from one level of the nervous system to another." (Nancy McWilliams, "Projection," Britannica, https://www.britannica.com/science/projection-psychology.)

‡ This phrase is a common slogan in the twelve-step recovery world. The original author of "You spot it, you got it" is unknown.

💭 Identify Your Projections

Instructions: Think of a person you don't like. They can be real or fictional, a person you know or a person you've never met. Think about the qualities about them that bother you and then be brutally honest with yourself: Is it possible that the thing you don't like about them is a quality you've disowned in yourself?

Disclaimer: Do not include abusers of any kind on this list.

Person or Type of Person I Don't Like	What Is It About Them That Bothers Me the Most?	Where in My Own Life Do I See This Quality or Fear This Quality?
My coworker Doug	Doug is loud, annoying, and makes dumb jokes.	If I am being honest, I'm probably loud and annoying sometimes, and I worry that I don't have a good sense of humor and people will judge me.
The mommy blogger who freely dances around their messy kitchen on TikTok	They aren't acting very mature, their kitchen is a mess, and they're setting a bad example for their children.	I'm worried that if everything is not perfect my life will fall apart, but the truth is, I wish I could be free to dance and not have everything spotless all the time.

Now that you've identified your projections, it's time to withdraw them. One of my favorite methods of projection withdrawal is called the "That's a little bit true" exercise. I'm not sure where it came from, but I am sure I did not invent it. This exercise allows you to microdose your undesirable qualities. For example, if I'm afraid that I'm an imposter (and who among us hasn't experienced imposter syndrome?), I would do the exercise like this:

Thing I Fear	Microdose of Truth
I'm afraid that I'm an imposter.	It's a little bit true that I'm an imposter.

If I'm afraid that if people really knew me, they wouldn't like me, the exercise would look like this:

Thing I Fear	Microdose of Truth
If they knew me, they wouldn't like me.	It's a little bit true that if people really knew me, some people wouldn't like me.

If you're a parent, you might say something like this:

Thing I Fear	Microdose of Truth
I'm afraid I am a bad parent.	It's a little bit true that sometimes I'm not the greatest parent in the world.

If you're willing to admit that embedded in your psyche is "a little bit" of icky truth, you no longer need to hide from yourself. Just like a microdose of a psychedelic isn't likely to send you careening off to Wonderland if safely ingested under medical care, a microdose of truth isn't likely to send you careening into a shame spiral.

💭 Withdraw Your Projections

Instructions: Fill in the chart with your fears about yourself. Then give yourself a microdose of truth by affirming, "It's a little bit true that . . ."

Thing I Fear	Microdose of Truth

Why is projection work important? If we're going to be connected to other people (a prerequisite for happiness), we need to be able to see them. "Seeing" them is impossible if we're constantly evading and projecting our own undesirable qualities. Narcissistic personality disorder (which is a very real phenomenon *and* a grossly overused term) is defined by the extreme and pervasive projection of self-hatred. Most of us do not fall into this category, but everyone, including you and me, projects onto others to a degree. Identifying and withdrawing our projections deactivates many of the trigger points that electrocute our sense of well-being.

In *The Dark Side of the Light Chasers,* author Debbie Ford wrote: "Imagine having a hundred different electrical outlets on your chest. Each outlet represents a different quality. The qualities we acknowledge and embrace have cover plates over them. They are safe: no electricity runs through them. But the qualities that are not okay with us, which we have not yet owned, do have a charge. So when others come along who act out one of these qualities they plug right into us. . . . Since we lie to ourselves about our own internal feelings, the only way we can find them is to see them in others."

The people who trigger us are a gold mine for self-development (assuming they are not objectively causing harm). A lesser-known location for accessing shadow content is likely sitting next to you, in front of you, or in your pocket right now. This is a place few dare to tread. That place is . . . wait for it . . . your internet browser history.

Gulp.

Internet Rabbit Holes:
The Surprising Place Your Shadow Hides

Where do you go when no one is looking? What YouTube videos do you delete from your history after viewing? How many hours did you *really* spend online stalking your ex last night? To be honest, I feel less vulnerable sharing my drug history than my browser history. Peering down internet rabbit holes can tell you a lot about the dark side of your psyche—if you are courageous enough to look.

Disclaimer: Not all your internet use reflects your shadow qualities. There are plenty of times when you need to wander around the web for legitimate reasons like work research, connecting with friends, or watching *Darrin's Dance Grooves*. These are not the times to which this section refers.

Disclaimer: This section is not specifically about online pornography (although if that's where you go online, feel free to name that in the spaces below). Pornography deserves its own chapter/book/series and cannot be covered adequately here. The only thing I'll say about porn is this: *sometimes* your porn preferences can be portals to your origin wounds. Food for thought.

❧ Your Secret Online Behaviors

Instructions: This exercise is to give you an understanding of yourself, not to shame you with your internet tangents, no matter how seemingly bizarre they may be. Be nice to yourself as you complete it.

1. The types of websites I go to most often are _____.

2. What is it about these sites that draws me in? (Fantasy, distraction, comparison, inspiration, voyeurism, education?) _____
_____.

3. The types of TV shows I like the most are _____.

4. What I like most about these shows is _____.

5. The most recent internet search I deleted was _____.

6. I would be embarrassed if anyone knew I liked to look at _____
_____.

7. One of my favorite things to search for online is _____.

8. My favorite celebrity or influencer to look at online is _____
_____.

9. What fascinates me about this person is _____.

10. One thing I look at online that makes me feel bad about myself is _____
_____.

11. I continue to look at things that make me feel bad because _____
_____.

12. I'm afraid if I unfollow people, _____
_____ would happen.

👣 Social Media Unfollow Challenge

Instructions: Pick one or two, or do all three suggestions below.

1. Unfollow (or mute) three social media accounts that make you feel bad about yourself.

2. Unfollow (or mute) another three social media accounts that make you feel bad about yourself.

3. Repeat steps 1 and 2 until you no longer see content that makes you feel bad about yourself.

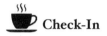 Check-In

Instructions: Either think about the following questions or write about them in your journal.

- What surprised you about the projection exercise?
- Which icky truth did you have the hardest time owning?
- What did your exploration of your online behavior reveal about you?
- How are you doing with your daily practice?

Observation: One takeaway from this work is:

_____

Recommendation: Something I can do with this information is:

_____

If you've made it this far, congratulations. You've ferreted out the sneaky untruths, biases, distortions, and projections hiding in your head. You've practiced holding multiple realities at the same time. You've given yourself permission to stop doing wellness practices that don't make sense for you, and you've recognized that you have feelings about things. You've also admitted to your secret online behaviors. Well done. There's one final shadow work showdown you'll face here—your relationship with money.

Money Shadows: Uncovering Hidden Beliefs That Keep You Stuck

If you're at a dinner party and raise the topic of sex, the conversation will be spirited, humorous, and lively. But if you raise the topic of *money*, heads bow, eyes avert, and awkward silence fills the room. Why are we so uncomfortable? The next two tasks* focus on your relationship with money and how money shadows (which include secret thoughts like *All rich people are evil* or *I feel guilty for having money*) can drive your financial decisions.

Money Shadows

Instructions: Fill in the following blanks. After you complete each line, decide whether this belief is serving you. If not, draw a line through it.

I am entitled to _____ because _____.

I don't deserve _____ because _____.

I should give money to _____ because _____.

I shouldn't give money to _____ because _____.

Rich people have money because _____.

Poor people don't have money because _____.

Don't ever spend money on/for _____.

Always spend money on/for _____.

Don't trust _____ with your money.

You can always trust _____ with your money.

Only rich people can _____.

Only poor people can _____.

If someone has _____, they must be rich.

If someone has _____, they must be poor.

---

* Both tasks adapted with permission from Kahler Financial Group. Rick Kahler, MS, CFP, CFT-I, CeFT, is a pioneer in integrating financial planning and psychology. I met him at an Internal Family Systems training, and he has been invaluable in helping my inner children calm their money tantrums.

The stupidest thing you can do with money is _____.

The smartest thing you can do with money is _____.

I could never afford to _____.

I will always be able to afford to _____.

You can always count on money to _____.

I believe money is _____.

Cleaning Up Your Money Mess

I wanted to tear up the following checklist and throw it at my financial adviser's head when he first gave it to me. You might be tempted to skip some or all of these. Don't. You may be tempted to beat yourself up for your answers. Revisit the self-compassion section if that happens. Consider the words of James Clear in *Atomic Habits*: "Every action you take is a vote for the type of person you wish to become."

Instructions: Complete the following chart. Commit to putting something in the action column, no matter how microscopic. If the only action you can stomach today is admitting you haven't dealt with this stuff yet, that 10,000 percent counts.

Question	Y/N	What's *One* Action (No Matter How Tiny) I'm Willing to Take *Today*?
Do you have a budget?		
Do you pay off your credit card balances every month?		
Have you delayed medical, dental, or eye exams?		
If you own a car, is it in need of maintenance, like new tires, oil, brakes, or repairs?		
Do you pay all your taxes on time (state, federal, etc.)?		

Question	Y/N	What's *One* Action (No Matter How Tiny) I'm Willing to Take *Today?*
Have you made loans to friends, family, coworkers, or anyone else for which the repayment is overdue?		
Have you borrowed items that you have not returned?		
Are you charging enough for your services or earning a wage reflective of your value?		
Is your living space organized and free of clutter?		
Are all your debt payments current (car, home, student loans, etc.)?		
Can you go on a vacation and not need to fund it by credit card?		
If you have any overdue bills, have you worked out a repayment plan with the creditor?		
Are you fully aware of your monthly income and expenses or confident that you live on less than you make?		

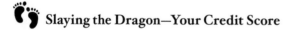

Slaying the Dragon—Your Credit Score

Instructions: If you don't know your credit score, do these things:

1. Decide to face it.
2. Take an action to find it. You can use a website like creditkarma.com or annualcreditreport.com or find it through your credit card company or bank.
3. Write a list of three choices for what you can do about your score if the number isn't good.

4. See which of the three choices feels easiest.

5. Do it.

Ugly truth is fertilizer for a beautiful life. If you feel stressed or overwhelmed at the idea of feeling your feelings, assessing your wellness practices, withdrawing your projections, and looking at your finances, I hear you. It takes time and energy to do these things. Shadow work can be uncomfortable and painful. But as you read earlier, there is no viable way to wriggle out of the human experience. As an unknown author aptly put it, "Despite the high cost of living, it remains popular."

When it comes to living, you have two options: consciously check the settings on your thought filters, or have your brain unconsciously do the filtering for you. With willingness to look under the hood of our beautiful but biased brains, we can feel more in charge of our own lives. As Carl Jung wrote, "Until you make the unconscious conscious it will direct your life and you will call it fate." As someone who spent decades directed by my unconscious, I can personally vouch that doing this work is easier than not doing it. Even the most artful dodges of reality did not protect me from the discomfort of humanity. I can promise that the discomfort of doing this work is exceedingly better than the discomfort that comes from avoiding it.

⚷ Bottom-Line Takeaways

- ▸ Shadow work is the process of developing self-awareness.
- ▸ At some point, most people are likely to tell themselves half-truths or untruths.
- ▸ Even the most popular wellness practices do not always work for all people in all situations.
- ▸ Feelings are physiological body sensations.
- ▸ Two (or more) conflicting things can be true at the same time.
- ▸ The human brain is biased. Everyone is biased to a degree.
- ▸ The places you secretly go online can tell you a lot about yourself.
- ▸ Projection is a way to avoid undesirable qualities in yourself.
- ▸ Facing your financial reality is preferable to hiding from it.

DOS AND DON'TS OF COMPASSIONATE SELF-AWARENESS

Do	Don't
Remember that all groups have the potential to be life-giving or life-draining.	Frantically obsess over your practices. If they work for you, great.
Allow yourself to toss or modify any wellness practices that don't feel right to you.	Force yourself to do any wellness practice just because it's trending on social media.
Remember that your brain does many things automatically.	Forget that you can help influence your brain in the direction you want to go.
Be compassionate with yourself as you navigate your wellness journey.	Tell yourself that self-compassion is dumb. There's hard science that shows self-compassion improves performance and decreases stress.

End-of-Level Challenge

Instructions: This is adapted from the tenth step of the twelve steps of Alcoholics Anonymous. You can do this exercise once, twice, or as often as needed to self-check and course correct. If you want to see yourself rapidly grow, try this exercise daily for the next thirty days.

Question to Ask Yourself	Y/N	Things to Consider
Did I experience resentment?		Of whom? Why? What does resentment feel like in my body? What's one action I can take *today* to help myself?
Did I experience jealousy?		Of whom? What's my jealousy trying to show me? What does jealousy feel like in my body? What's one action I can take *today* to help myself?
Did I lie to myself today?		What was the lie? What is the truth? Am I willing to own this truth? What's one action I can take *today* to help myself?

Question to Ask Yourself	Y/N	Things to Consider
Am I keeping a secret today?		What is the secret? Is there anyone I'm willing to tell? What are the consequences of keeping this secret? What is one action I can take *today* to help myself? *(Completing this chart counts!)*
Is it possible I made any assumptions today?		What was the assumption? What was the event that triggered the assumption? What's another explanation besides the story I'm telling myself? What is one action I can take *today* to help myself?
Did I do anything to look at my financial health today?		What is my belief about my finances? What am I afraid will happen if I look at my finances? What's one tiny action I can take *today* to address my finances? What is the consequence of not addressing my finances?

Congratulations! You've reached the end of this part. Use the space below for final observations and recommendations:

Observations:

_____

_____

_____

Recommendations:

_____

_____

_____

PART 5

Probable Impossibilities

Getting the Life You Want

This final part is a palate cleanser for the heavier stuff you've waded through thus far. Here, you'll focus on how to reclaim your sense of balance, creativity, and playfulness.

Suddenly something that wasn't even a possibility became a reality.

—Shawn Achor

don't enjoy puzzles. It seems ludicrous to rip apart a perfectly good picture and then be forced to spend hours hunched over a table trying to put it back together. Admittedly, my personal dislike of this activity makes me an outlier—puzzles are a multibillion-dollar industry with global competitions, festivals, and conferences. Jigsaw puzzle enthusiasts even have a special name—*dissectologists*. To me, putting together a puzzle feels like a punishment. For others, puzzles are a beloved way to play.

What does this have to do with you?

You may not be a puzzle person, a video game person, or a sportsball person, but play is not optional if you want wholeness and happiness. If the thought of playfulness in *any* form feels like an impossible task, the next section shows you why play is necessary, why it can feel off-putting, and what you can do to bring it back into your life.

Why Play Is Necessary

Play is not a waste of time. "Over the last 30 years, science has shown that play is very productive for humans at any age; we need play to keep our brains flexible, ward off depression, sustain optimism, and sharpen our social-emotional skills."[*] What do scientists and researchers mean when they talk about "play"? I like the explanation by Bernard Suits in the book *The Grasshopper: Games, Life and Utopia*, in which Suits defines playing a game as "the voluntary attempt to overcome unnecessary obstacles."

⛏—O Play is any activity "freely sought and pursued solely for the sake of individual or group enjoyment."[†]

Important things to know about play:

▸ Play does not need to have any practical applications.

---

[*] "Play for Adults," National Institute for Play, https://www.nifplay.org/play-for-you/make-play-part-of-an-adult-life.

[†] "Play," *APA Dictionary of Psychology*, American Psychological Association, https://dictionary.apa.org/play.

- Play does not need to have a purpose.
- Play does not need to produce a product.
- Regardless of the activity, if it's not fun for the participant, it doesn't count as play.

💭 My Beliefs About Play

Instructions: Fill in the blanks with the first thought that comes to your mind.

1. The last time I felt playful I was _____.

2. The last time I let myself play, I played _____.

3. When I see kids play, I feel _____.

4. When I think about playing myself, I _____.

5. Play for kids is _____.

6. Play for adults is _____.

7. Play for me is _____.

8. I can't let myself play because _____.

9. I'm worried if I start playing I will _____.

10. What I believed about play when I was a kid was _____.

11. My favorite thing to play as a kid was _____.

12. My favorite toy as a kid was _____.

13. On a scale of one to ten (one being the least and ten, the most) how comfortable am I with play? _____

14. On a scale of one to ten (one being the least and ten, the most) how important do I think play is for adults? _____

A quick web search for "science of play" yields millions of articles, studies, and scholarly journal writings on why play is necessary for both child *and* adult development. The next exercise is an assignment I often give skeptical clients who are not convinced that play is as important to their mental and physical well-being as sunshine and fresh air.

👣 The Science of Play (Listen, Read, Watch)

Instructions: Of the three resources listed below, pick one and either listen to, read, or watch it. Give yourself bonus points if you do all three.

1. **Listen:** The *TED Radio Hour* has an episode called "Press Play." It provides a fascinating overview of "how all forms of amusement—from tossing a ball to video games—can make us smarter, saner and more collaborative."[*] Google it, and listen to it. Then write your takeaways in your notebook or journal.

2. **Read:** Psych Central has an article called "The Importance of Play for Adults" by Saya Des Marais, MSW.[†] Google it, and read it. Then write your takeaways in your notebook or journal.

3. **Watch:** TEDMED has a talk called "The Power of Play" by Jill Vialet. Google it, and watch it. Then write your takeaways in your notebook or journal.

Ready, Set, Play

Play has broad definitions and expressions. Dr. Stuart Brown, founder of the National Institute for Play, puts it this way: "As we grow up, we develop strong preferences for certain types of play over others. One person's fun is another person's boredom." Dr. Brown coined the phrase *play personalities* to describe eight primary styles of play. Some people identify strongly with one; others find themselves with a combination of play personalities.

---

[*] "Press Play," *TED Radio Hour*, March 27, 2015, https://www.npr.org/programs/ted-radio-hour/390249044.

[†] Saya Des Marais, MSW, "The Importance of Play for Adults," Psych Central, November 10, 2022, https://psych central.com/blog/the-importance-of-play-for-adults.

♥ The Eight Play Personalities

Instructions: The table below summarizes Dr. Brown's eight play personalities with examples of activities to match the personality.

Step 1: Circle the play personality that represents you most.

Step 2: Underline the play personality you identify with second-most.

Step 3: Put a check mark next to the play personality that you identify with third-most.

	Play Personality	Description/Activities
	1. The joker	The joker play personality loves laughter. Joker-inspired activities include watching stand-up comedy, participating in improv classes, playing fun (and harmless) practical jokes, or making silly videos.
	2. The kinesthete	The kinesthete play personality loves movement. Kinesthete-inspired activities include dancing, swimming, rock climbing, yoga, martial arts, or sports. Important to note: If your primary motivation to do an activity is because you want to burn calories or tone your thighs, that activity does not count as play.
	3. The explorer	The explorer play personality loves new things. Explorer-inspired activities include trying new restaurants, discovering new places in your city, traveling, reading, or attempting to do anything new and different.
	4. The competitor	The competitor play personality loves (harmless) opposition. Competitor-inspired activities include playing games with rules and rituals like chess or board games, playing video games, participating in team sports, and competing in races.
	5. The director	The director play personality loves planning. Director-inspired activities include creating and executing events, organizing meetups, directing plays, or hosting parties. Note: If you are planning and executing events out of obligation (or if you don't enjoy doing it), it does not count as play.
	6. The collector	The collector play personality loves found objects. Collector-inspired activities include thrift store and vintage shop hunting, storing and displaying found objects, finding interesting rocks or crystals, or searching for rare books.

Play Personality	Description/Activities
7. The storyteller	The storyteller play personality loves narratives. Storyteller-inspired activities include watching movies, going to see live theater, reading, and participating in anything to do with character arcs and development.
8. The creator/artist	The creator/artist play personality likes making things. Creator/artist-inspired activities include crafting, making art, composing music, singing, designing or wearing fashion, putting things together, or participating in any activity in which something that didn't previously exist now exists.

Because creativity is an essential component to wholeness, the next section focuses on helping you unlock your sense of creativity (even if you don't think you are a creative person).

Let's Play

Instructions: Now that you've identified your top three play personalities, it's time to take them out for a spin. Fill in the table below.

My Play Personality	One Activity I'll Try	Did I Do It? (Y/N)	Thoughts
1.			
2.			
3.			

 **Check-In**

Instructions: Either think about the following questions or write about them in your journal.

- ▸ Have your thoughts on the importance of play changed? Why or why not?
- ▸ How was the experience of playing for you? If you haven't tried a play activity, consider going back and picking one to complete.
- ▸ How are you doing with your daily practice?

Observation: One takeaway from this work is:

_____

Recommendation: Something I can do with this information is:

_____

Creativity and Safety

Authors, scientists, researchers, artists, and experts across multiple disciplines all agree: creativity is good for us. Few would argue that creativity is *not* a high-flying wellness superhero. We often fantasize about what life would be like if we had more money, more beauty, or more things, but when was the last time you imagined what life would be like if it included more creativity?

Creative Possibilities

Instructions: Read the following list of all the benefits of creativity and then fill in the blanks.

▸ Creativity is an antidepressant.

One thing I could do if I felt happier would be _____

_____.

▸ Creativity increases cognitive function.

One thing I could do if I could think clearer would be _____

_____.

▸ Creativity helps with problem-solving.

One thing I could do if I could find quicker solutions would be _____

_____.

▸ Creativity promotes connection and collaboration.

One thing I could do if I felt more connected to other people would be _____

_____.

▸ Creativity alleviates stress and burnout.

One thing I could do if I felt more relaxed would be _____

_____.

▸ Creativity is an immune system booster.

One thing I could do if I felt better physically would be _____

_____.

▸ Creativity improves emotional resilience.

One thing I could do if I felt more emotionally grounded would be _____

_____.

There are many reasons why people feel blocked creatively, with fear topping the list. Creativity—in any form—can spark inspiration in some and anxiety in others. *Big Magic* author Elizabeth Gilbert notes, "Fear will always be triggered by creativity, because creativity asks you to enter realms that are of uncertain outcomes and *fear hates uncertain outcomes.*" The benefits to creativity are nearly limitless, but for some people, the idea of practicing creativity feels nearly impossible. If you fall into that category, remind yourself what the incomparable Ted Lasso says: "You say impossible, but all I hear is 'I'm possible.'"

As you read in part 1, your brain needs to feel safe to make decisions and stay out of freeze mode. Anything that is too much, too fast, or too soon—even good things—can put your nervous system into a state of freezy-stuckness. My friend, trauma therapist Crystle Lampitt, says, "It's hard to be creative when your brain is shut down. Creativity requires your brain to feel safe enough to access its creative functions."

From an evolutionary standpoint, making decisions was a high-stakes endeavor. If you made a wrong move, took a wrong path, or interacted with the wrong person, you would die or be cast out from your tribe. And as Joseph Chilton Pearce noted: "To live a creative life, we must lose our fear of being wrong." These feelings of danger and fear are further amplified if you don't feel safe to look silly. If I didn't feel safe to look completely ridiculous, it would be impossible to practice aerial arts, which is my favorite nonwork activity. I have great respect and appreciation for all the adults at my studio. After our efforts to look pretty while flopping about during an aerial harness class, one of my circus friends, Madison Nicole, author of *The Immortality Trials*, observed, "We often get told that if we don't start something when we are a kid, then we missed out and that it's too late. The reality is, you can start anything at any age. There is so much value in creative movement spaces where you can be a beginner with other adults and be vulnerable."

If you don't think of yourself as a creative person, the next set of exercises are appropriate for you to try. If you *do* think of yourself as creative, but struggle to give yourself permission to create, these exercises help you dismantle the barriers between you and your creations.

💭 My Barriers to Creativity

Instructions: Look at the following list of creative barriers. In the spaces, rank them from one to five, with one being the least scary and five being the scariest.

- ▸ Creativity requires **vulnerability**. ____
- ▸ Creativity requires **failure**. ____
- ▸ Creativity requires **decision-making**. ____

> ▸ Creativity requires **curiosity**. ____
> ▸ Creativity requires **discomfort**. ____

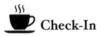 **Creating Safety**

Instructions: Each of the five barriers listed is described in the following pages with a corresponding task. You can start with whichever barrier you labeled least scary (1) and work your way up to what you labeled scariest (5). If you don't like the suggested task, feel free to make up one of your own.

Creative Barrier: Vulnerability

Why it's scary: When you are vulnerable, you are open and exposed to getting hurt.

What you can do: Keep your creative efforts private so you aren't vulnerable.

Suggested task: Decorate a cake or cookie and then eat it.

☕ **Check-In**

Instructions: Either think about the following questions or write about them in your journal.

> ▸ Did you try the vulnerability task?
> ▸ How did it go?

Creative Barrier: Failure

Why it's scary: Failure creates stories of shame and unworthiness.

What you can do: Set out to fail intentionally. If your goal is to fail intentionally and then you fail, you've succeeded in your failure efforts. Sound confusing? That's the idea. The ensuing confusion allows your creativity to sneak out of its cage.

Suggested task: With your nondominant hand (if you are right-handed, use your left hand; if you are left-handed, use your right hand), take a giant marker, chubby crayon, or piece of chalk and draw for five minutes. Set a timer. Your results will be a big mess. Feel free to laugh and repeat.

 Check-In

Instructions: Either think about the following questions or write about them in your journal.

- ▸ Did you try the failure task?
- ▸ How did it go?

Creative Barrier: Decision-Making

Why it's scary: Decision-making feels impossible and dangerous when your brain is overwhelmed.

What you can do: Minimize the decisions you need to make.

Suggested task: Use the three circles below, or draw three circles in your notebook or journal. Doodle in each of the three circles.*

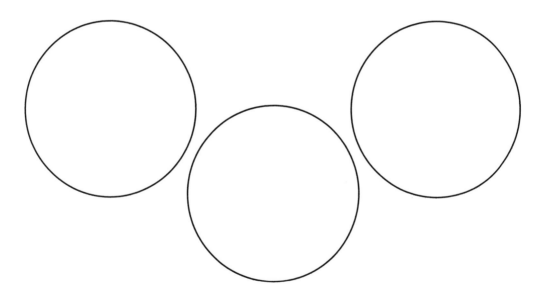

---

*This exercise is an adaptation of mandala art. "Many people find the drawing or colouring of a mandala to be meditative. As they focus on colouring in the patterns of the form, they relax, their mind grows quiet, and they may enter into a spiritual space. The very nature of drawing a mandala is therapeutic and symbolic." ("Mandalas and Art Therapy," Hoffman Institute, https://www.hoffmaninstitute.co.uk/mandalas-art-therapy.)

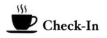 **Check-In**

Instructions: Either think about the following questions or write about them in your journal.

- ▸ Did you try the decision-making task?
- ▸ How did it go?

Creative Barrier: Curiosity

Why it's scary: Curiosity means you don't know what will happen next.

What you can do: Practice curiosity in small, safe doses with no potential consequences.

Suggested task: Take an everyday object (a glass, a pillow, a plate, or anything else you have laying around), and see if you can come up with ten possible uses for the object besides its intended function.* For example, other uses for a pen might be a weapon, a hair accessory, or a fidget toy.

 **Check-In**

Instructions: Either think about the following questions or write about them in your journal.

- ▸ Did you try the curiosity task?
- ▸ How did it go?

Creative Barrier: Discomfort

Why it's scary: Our brains often equate discomfort with danger.

What you can do: Uncouple discomfort from danger.

---

*This is an exercise often used in improv classes. It is also the basis for a business exercise called the 30 Circles Test, in which you need to come up with thirty different ways a circle can be turned into a recognizable object.

Suggested task: Get into an uncomfortable (but not harmful) body position. It can be standing on one leg until you feel uncomfortable, sitting on your feet, holding a plank, stretching until you feel your hamstrings get tight, or any position that you wouldn't want to stay in for more than a minute or two. Set a timer for three minutes. Look around the room, and notice that you are still safe. Say to yourself, preferably out loud, "I am safe. I am uncomfortable, and I am still safe."

 **Check-In**

Instructions: Either think about the following questions or write about them in your journal.

- Did you try the discomfort task?
- How did it go?

To sum it up:

Creativity Barrier	Why It's Scary	What You Can Do
Creativity requires **vulnerability**.	Vulnerability opens you up to being hurt.	Keep your creative projects to yourself.
Creativity requires **failure**.	Failure creates stories of shame and unworthiness.	Set out to fail intentionally.
Creativity requires **decision-making**.	Decision-making feels impossible when your brain is overwhelmed.	Minimize the decisions you'll need to make.
Creativity requires **curiosity**.	Curiosity means you don't know what will happen next.	Make the unknown more known.
Creativity requires **discomfort**.	Our brains often equate discomfort with danger.	Uncouple discomfort from danger.

What's Your Creativity Personality?

When most people hear the word *creativity*, they immediately think of things like painting, drawing, or dancing or other artistic endeavors. Creativity and business expert David Parrish observed, "Some people will say they are 'not creative,' meaning that they are not talented artistically, even though they might be ingenious engineers, innovative farmers, or inventive educationalists. As one of my clients, JD, an artistic day trader, put it, 'Creating is communicating.' Ironically, many people who are indeed very communicative don't relate to the word 'creativity.'" Working with clay or playing the cello are not your only choices if you want to play with creativity. Just as with the play personalities you read about in the previous section, there are also different types of creativity personalities. Knowing your creativity personality expands your range of creative outlets and increases the likelihood that you will attempt to be creative.

♥ The Eight Creativity Personalities

Instructions: There likely are limitless types of creative personalities, but I've identified eight for you to work with in this exercise.

Step 1: Circle the creativity personality that represents you most.
Step 2: Underline the creativity personality you identify with second-most.
Step 3: Put a check mark next to the creativity personality that you identify with third-most.

	Creativity Personality	Description/Activities
	1. The maker	The maker loves putting together different elements to form something new. Maker-inspired activities include crafts, building things, making collages, knitting, creating visual arts, building with LEGO, sewing, and cooking.

Creativity Personality	Description/Activities
2. The composer	The composer loves to put ideas to paper. Composer-inspired activities include writing stories or poems, journaling, writing music, designing buildings, mapmaking, drafting business plans and marketing strategies, penning written content, or creating social media content.
3. The seer	The seer loves to bring the composer's creations to life. Seer-inspired activities include shooting videos, creating digital content for social media, making movies, taking photos, teaching, executing a marketing strategy, or launching a business.
4. The imagineer	The imagineer loves to participate in the worlds created by the composer and the seer. Imagineer-inspired activities include watching movies, reading, listening to music, admiring architecture, or going to museums or art shows.
5. The social engineer	The social engineer loves to create connections. Events are the social engineer's canvas, and people are their paints. Social engineer–inspired activities include planning parties, organizing get-togethers, creating scavenger hunts, planning weddings or showers, hosting book clubs, or creating networking opportunities for people.
6. The naturalist	The naturalist loves the outdoors and bringing the outdoors inside. Naturalist-inspired activities include landscaping, gardening, using essential oils, growing herbs, planting flowers and other plants, and cooking.
7. The somatic	The somatic loves using their physical body. Somatic-inspired activities include dancing, bodybuilding, hiking, playing sports, playing music, or doing yoga.
8. The problem-solver	The problem-solver loves to create solutions. Problem-solver-inspired activities include brainstorming, list-making, putting together puzzles, figuring out escape rooms or murder mysteries, or playing collaborative games.

👣 Time to Create

Instructions: Now that you've identified your top three creative personalities, it's time to take them out for a spin. Fill in the table on the next page.

My Creative Personality	One Activity I'll Try	Did I Do It? (Y/N)	Thoughts
1.			
2.			
3.			

 **Check-In**

Instructions: Either think about the following questions or write about them in your journal.

- ▸ Have your thoughts on the importance of creativity changed? Why or why not?
- ▸ How was the experience of creating for you? If you haven't tried a creative activity, consider going back and picking one to complete.
- ▸ How are you doing with your daily practice?

Observation: One takeaway from this work is:

_____

Recommendation: Something I can do with this information is:

_____

The Power of Visualization

One of the most useful ways to practice both playfulness and creativity—no matter what you identify as your play and creativity personalities—is to practice the art of visualization. An article on ScienceDaily put it this way: "Researchers have found that self-guided positive imagery training can successfully combat negative emotions in our daily lives." The benefits of visualization are not limited to your emotional experience. That same article notes, "This tool is so powerful that it also changes the way our brain functions."[*]

How can visualization change the way your brain functions?

"When you have a thought, it triggers the same cascade of neurochemicals, regardless of whether you are thinking about the past, present, or future. Your brain is stimulated the same way whether you're physically performing an action or simply visualizing it happen in your mind's eye."[†] The ability to create mental pictures is a useful skill for cultivating happiness. As philosopher Immanuel Kant put it [italics mine], "Happiness is an ideal not of *reason* but of *imagination*."

The next set of exercises help you strengthen your visualization muscles. If you identify as someone with aphantasia (the inability to visualize), you can search online for images to use in lieu of creating mental pictures. The first exercise is one of the most common exercises used in psychotherapy and comes from the solution-focused therapy framework.

♥ Visualization Exercise 1: The Miracle Question

Instructions: Either think about the following question or write it down in your journal.

If you woke up tomorrow and your biggest problem was miraculously solved, what would the day look like? Describe the day in as much detail as possible, including where you would

---

[*] Frontiers, "Teach Yourself Everyday Happiness with Imagery Training," ScienceDaily, February 24, 2017, https://www.sciencedaily.com/releases/2017/02/170224111813.htm.

[†] Melody Wilding, LMSW, "The Complete Guide to Visualization for Logical and Rational People," Medium, April 10, 2018, https://betterhumans.pub/the-complete-guide-to-visualization-for-logical-and-rational-people -f1dadd10029f.

go, what you would do, how you would dress, what you would eat, with whom you would spend time, what you would listen to or watch, and how it would feel. You can include things like how you would start and end the day, what you would do for work (if you work), what you would see when you look in the mirror, and how you would be treated by the people around you.

Visualization Exercise 2: Home Screen Inspiration

Instructions: One of the easiest ways to practice visualization is to use a tool that you access all day, every day—your phone. Find an inspiring photo and save it as your home screen background. It can be someone doing something you want to do, a location you want to visit, or anything else that would be useful to look at.

Visualization Exercise 3: The Do/Be/Have List

Instructions: Create a do/be/have list. Write down ten things you want to *do*, ten things you want to *be*, and ten things you want to *have*. Use the space below, or write in your journal.

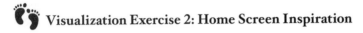

What Do I Want to *Do*?	How Do I Want to *Be*?	What Do I Want to *Have*?
1.	1.	1.
2.	2.	2.
3.	3.	3.

What Do I Want to *Do?*	How Do I Want to *Be?*	What Do I Want to *Have?*
4.	4.	4.
5.	5.	5.
6.	6.	6.
7.	7.	7.
8.	8.	8.
9.	9.	9.
10.	10.	10.

❧ Visualization Exercise 4: You Are Safe

Instructions: This is a technique based on a trauma healing modality called somatic experiencing. Find a comfortable and quiet spot to sit or lie down. You can use the following instructions or modify this exercise in any way that makes sense for you. The safety affirmations can be said out loud (preferably) or inside your head. This exercise is not designed to relax you or make uncomfortable sensations more comfortable. This is intended to help you access a sense of safety.

Disclaimer: If you are currently unsafe, do *not* do this exercise. If you have pain or a medical condition, skip the step associated with it.

Step 1: Notice your head. Slowly move it side to side. Then say, "My head is safe right now."

Step 2: Notice your neck and shoulders. Slowly move or stretch them. Then say, "My neck and shoulders are safe right now."

Step 3: Notice your arms and chest. Slowly move or stretch them. Then say, "My arms and chest are safe right now."

Step 4: Notice your core. Slowly move or stretch it. Then say, "My core is safe right now."

Step 5: Notice your hips and legs. Slowly move or stretch them. Then say, "My hips and legs are safe right now."

Step 6: Notice your feet and hands. Slowly move or stretch them. Then say, "My feet and hands are safe right now."

Step 7: Do a full-body scan, from the top of your head down to your toes. Slowly move or stretch your whole body. Then say, "My body is here. My body is safe right now."

☕ Check-In

Instructions: Either think about the following questions or write about them in your journal.

- Are there any elements of your miracle day that you can bring into your current life?
- How was the experience of visualizing for you? If you haven't tried a visualization activity, consider going back and picking one to complete.
- How are you doing with your daily practice?

Observation: One takeaway from this work is:

_____

Recommendation: Something I can do with this information is:

The Myth of Work/Life Balance

Work/life balance is hailed as the panacea for happiness. The second-most common question[*] I hear when working with clients is, "How do I get more balance in my life?" The message many of us learned to believe is, "When I have more work/life balance, I will feel better."

But there's a big problem with this message.

What if the reason we struggle to find work/life balance is that, deep down, there's a part of us that knows we do *not* want or need it? We think if we achieve balance, we'll find our way to happiness and health. There's no doubt that we live in a world where struggle, overwhelm, burnout, anxiety, and a 24/7 ambush of bad news are part of daily life. But balance is *not* the vehicle to get you where you want to go.

Why? There are three primary reasons why balance is not a helpful goal:

1. **Balance and choice can't coexist.**

   Picture a tightrope walker in a circus. They're perfectly balanced. But because all their energy needs to focus on maintaining the precision necessary for balance, their choices are extremely limited.

   What this means for you: If you have a perfectly balanced work/life situation, you are no longer able to choose where to invest your extra time or energy, nor are you able to choose your priorities.

---

[*] As I mentioned in the introduction to this book, the number one most-asked question is, "Am I crazy?" to which the answer is always a resounding *no*. There is no such thing as a "crazy" person. Even the most extreme mental health symptoms make sense in context.

2. **Balance and freedom can't coexist.**

Think of that same tightrope walker. They must have full control of their movements and their apparatus to stay safe and successfully execute their act. Exploration and spontaneity are not available. The state of balance that is exhilarating to watch as a spectator is limiting to the performer's freedom.

What this means for you: If you have a perfectly balanced work/life situation, you are no longer free to be curious or spontaneous.

3. **Balance and passion can't coexist.**

Passion is an extreme emotion. A perfectly balanced state of being is incompatible with passion. Imagine that tightrope walker going home to their partner and requesting a perfectly balanced intimacy session where each partner gets the same amount of time. Boring.

What this means for you: If you have a perfectly balanced work/life situation, passion is no longer an option. If everyone gets equal access to your time, no one, including you, gets full access to your gifts, energy, or enthusiasm.

Most people would say they value choice, freedom, and passion, yet these values are incompatible with balance. *So if balance isn't the goal*, you might be wondering, *what target should I aim for?* The answer to that question is *boundaries*.

⚷ When we say we want more work/life *balance*, what we really mean is we need more work/life *boundaries*.

Work/Life Boundaries

At the extreme end of the spectrum, people who struggle with work/life boundaries are identified as workaholics. Although the term *workaholic* gets tossed around casually and even jokingly, true workaholism is a serious problem and can have extreme physical and emotional consequences. In his book *Chained to the Desk*, author and psychotherapist Bryan Robinson describes workaholism as "an obsessive-compulsive disorder that manifests itself through self-imposed demands, an inability to regulate work habits, and overindulgence in work to the exclusion of most other life activities."

The next section is a boundary boot camp to help you toss the impossible idea of work/life balance and replace it with work/life *boundaries*. If you are concerned about severe workaholism, you may benefit from seeking professional support.

👣 Boundary Boot Camp

Instructions: Read through the following "workout." Start with the warm-up first, move to the workout, and then finish with the cooldown.

Note: You do not have to do everything at once. Feel free to do things one at a time or switch up the order if that makes more sense for your situation.

WARM-UP

Exercise	How to Do It	Date Completed
Time inventory	Use your phone's Notes app or write down in your journal everything you do during the day. Set a timer, and every thirty minutes, jot down your activities. By the end of the day, you will have a good picture of where time can be saved and where time could be put to different uses. Do this for one week.	
Decision-fatigue prevention	Decision-fatigue saps energy you need for more important things. Minimize the knucklehead decisions you need to make for the week by choosing one outfit to wear every day, the same meals to eat every day, let Spotify choose your music for you, and eliminate or automate as many decisions as possible.	

WORKOUT

Exercise	How to Do It	Date Completed
Willingness	You may not be willing to confront your boss, but maybe you are willing to shave an hour off your twelve-hour workday. You may not be willing to stop checking emails at night, but maybe you're willing to spend an hour of tech-free time with your family. Pick three things you're willing to do this week. Do them.	
Clothing change	If you work from home, it's especially difficult for your brain to differentiate between "I'm at work" and "I'm at home." Whether you work from home or outside the home, change your clothes at the end of your workday. This helps train your brain to shift into "not working" mode. Do this for one week.	

COOLDOWN

Exercise	How to Do It	Date Completed
Digital detox	Using your phone's display settings, turn your screen to grayscale. The lack of colors will help your brain not feel as compelled to scroll. You might feel frustrated by the lack of colors. This digital detox period usually will not last more than a day or two before your brain adjusts.	
Spending detox	It can be easy to mindlessly spend. Close Amazon; make a list and only purchase things one time a week; and if you're going to make a Target run, let a friend know what you're planning to buy beforehand and then check in with them when you leave.	

 **Check-In**

Instructions: Either think about the following questions or write about them in your journal.

▸ Has your view on work/life balance shifted? Why or why not?

- How was the experience of doing the work/life boot camp? If you haven't tried any of the boundary activities, consider going back and picking one to complete.
- How are you doing with your daily practice?

Observation: One takeaway from this work is:

_____

Recommendation: Something I can do with this information is:

_____

Inner Balance

Work/life balance is a myth—but creating a balance between *giving* and *taking* is a necessity. If you don't balance giving time and energy to others with taking time and energy for yourself, you'll quickly lose your footing. Too much giving creates burnout and self-abandonment, and too much taking creates rumination and self-indulgence. Put another way:

🔑 Acts of service without self-care create self-denial and resentment.

🔑 Acts of self-care without service create self-indulgence and lack of perspective.

Service	Self-Care
Service to others is part of being a responsible global citizen. But if you're a people-pleaser whose entire sense of worth comes from being of service to others, doing more acts of service is going to amplify the problem.	Taking time for self-care is essential to keep your emotional tank full. Self-care prevents resentment and burnout. But if you're a self-indulger whose focus is constantly centered on yourself, doing more acts of self-care is going to amplify the problem.

🪷 Service and Self-Care Inventory

Instructions: See the scale below. Extreme givers fall on one end of the scale, and extreme takers fall on the other. Without shaming yourself or beating yourself up, put a mark on the scale where you think you land. If you land more toward the Self-Denial end of the scale, do the following exercise for self-deniers. If you fall more toward the Self-Indulgence end of the scale, do the exercise for self-indulgers. If you are not sure where you fall, or if you fall somewhere in the middle, you can do both.

Instructions: Follow the steps below.

Step 1: For all the tasks in the following chart, mark down how uncomfortable you feel doing it, with one being the most comfortable and five being the most uncomfortable.

Step 2: Pick the easiest task (marked one), and do it. In the space provided or in your journal, write down how it went.

Step 3: Repeat with the second-most comfortable task, and continue until all the exercises are complete.

Task	Rating (One to Five)	Notes
Say no to someone who asks you for help with something.		
Take yourself out (solo) for a nice meal.		
Send yourself a gift.		
Send something back. This can be sending back a coffee or restaurant order, or you can physically return an item you purchased to the store.		
Ask someone for help with something.		

Instructions: Follow the steps on the next page.

Step 1: For each task in the chart below, mark down how uncomfortable you feel doing it, with one being the most comfortable and five being the most uncomfortable.

Step 2: Pick the easiest task (marked one), and do it. In the space provided or in your journal, write down how it went.

Step 3: Repeat with the second-most comfortable task, and continue until all the exercises are complete.

Task	Rating (One to Five)	Notes
Do an act of service for someone. This can be donating money, holding a door open, or helping someone with something.		
Say something nice to someone.		
Give a gift to someone.		
Volunteer. This can be formal, through a community service organization, or informal, by volunteering to help a friend or coworker.		
Make a list of ten things you feel grateful for. If there any people involved with your gratitude items, send them a card (or a text) thanking them.		

☕ Check-In

Instructions: Either think about the following questions or write about them in your journal.

- ▸ What feelings came up for you with the self-denier/self-indulgence scale?
- ▸ How was the experience of doing the exercises? If you haven't tried any of the activities, consider going back and picking one to complete.
- ▸ How are you doing with your daily practice?

Observation: One takeaway from this work is:

_____

Recommendation: Something I can do with this information is:

_____

Life Expectations: A Year in Quarters

For this final section, we'll uncover the reason New Year's resolutions fail—and how you can take back the wheel of your life and avoid the cycle of resolve, relapse, repeat. You're not alone if you've long abandoned even the sincerest resolutions by the time chocolate hearts and teddy bears make their annual appearance. Why? It's not because you're unmotivated, and it's not because you're lazy. New Year's resolutions fail because if you're like most people, you've likely spent November and December slammed with obligations. The energy required to stick to New Year's resolutions is annihilated by the demands of the holiday season. The expectations you put on yourself in January are incongruent with your capacity. You wouldn't expect your car to make a cross-country trip on a quarter tank of gas, yet we do this to ourselves every time we set a resolution in January.

But there's an alternative.

What if you divided the year into quarters and approached your life like a business? Companies divide the year into quarters, and set quarterly goals and sales targets based on the flow of the calendar year. Instead of setting New Year's resolutions in January, setting New Year's resolutions in *April* makes your resolutions *much* more likely to stick.

I'll explain.

If you're reading this book, you likely fall into the category of people for whom the following annual breakdown applies.

ANNUAL BREAKDOWN

Quarter	What's Happening
Q1 (January to March)	After months of stress, holiday demands, and overindulging, you stand up and declare that you are finished drinking, eating, spending, scrolling, or whatever your thing is. You resolve to make sweeping changes. Then, when you return to old habits, you feel shame and beat yourself up. Before you know it, Valentine's Day rolls around with its entourage of heart-shaped chocolates and candy. At this point, you reason with yourself, *Why bother trying to stick to resolutions?* Plus, if you live in a cold climate, this is an especially poor time of year to try for five A.M. runs in the park.
Q2 (April to June)	The diet industry shifts into high marketing gear in the spring. Suddenly, you realize summer is coming and that you need to get your "summer body"* or something bad will happen. With renewed vigor fueled by warmer days and later sunsets, you vow to re-up those long-forgotten resolutions. *All bodies are "summer bodies." The marketing arm of the diet industry thrives on making us feel bad about ourselves.
Q3 (July to September)	Summer is in full swing, and depending on your situation, you may have kids' activities, barbecues and picnics, or traveling. This is the last chunk of time before school starts back up, so if you have kids, you are likely frantic, and if you don't, you might have other activities clamoring for your time.
Q4 (October to December)	Holiday season. Cue scary music. Did you know that the holiday season is to therapists what tax season is to accountants? By mid-November, you're likely short on time, short on cash, racing around your life forgetting all those boundary-setting skills you learned about on TikTok, staying up too late, and telling yourself, "It's fine. I'll fix this all in January." Then New Year's Eve rolls up with its glittery promises of new beginnings, and the cycle repeats.

If you look at the annual breakdown, you'll notice that April is when you are most likely to have the energy to stick to new goals. Rather than spending your first quarter setting expectations beyond your capacity, that time is best spent taking inventory of what went wrong (and what went right) the previous year, focusing on recharging your batteries, and recovering from the fourth-quarter madness. For this next exercise, you create your own annual breakdown—but with realistic, achievable, and calendar-appropriate expectations.

Actionable Tool:
Quarterly Boundary Prioritization

JAN-MAR

Catch your breath, take inventory of what worked last year.

JUL-SEP

Summer means different priorities for families.

APR-JUN

Now is the time to start a new routine/ make changes.

OCT-DEC

Hang on for dear life.

Setting Your Yearly Expectations

Instructions: You can't always control what life throws at you, and sometimes circumstances obliterate even the most thoughtfully constructed life plans, but assuming you are in a position where choice is available, do your best to map out a year's worth of goals, keeping in mind that April to May is the quarter when you likely will have the most amount of energy.

Quarter	My Realistic Expectations
Q1 (January to March)	
Q2 (April to June)	

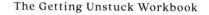

Quarter	My Realistic Expectations
Q3 (July to September)	
Q4 (October to December)	

A Note About Time

We all have a finite amount of time to live out our Earth journeys. There will never be enough time to do everything you "need" to do, let alone everything you want to do.* Moreover, there will never be enough time to explore and discover everything you're capable of doing. For everything to which you give your yes, there are countless things to which you must give your no. Every life path chosen means countless paths left behind. The limitations of time and space render it not only appropriate, but *necessary* to recognize there will be choices you didn't get to make and things you didn't get to do. Acceptance is not always popular, but nevertheless it is a powerful medicine that propels us forward. Refusing to accept the past means we likely will stay stuck there.

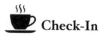 **Check-In**

Instructions: Either think about the following questions or write about them in your journal.

---

*Libraries make me sad. I will never have enough time to read all the books and ingest and absorb all the available knowledge. Anyone else relate?

▸ How did the quarterly exercise change your view of your life expectations?

▸ If you haven't tried the quarterly exercise, consider going back and jotting down at least one or two notes per quarter to try.

▸ Are there things you haven't allowed yourself to feel?

▸ How are you doing with your daily practice?

Observation: One takeaway from this work is:

_____

Recommendation: Something I can do with this information is:

_____

Final Thoughts

A discussion of play, creativity, and balance would be incomplete without a mention of spirituality. I'm no spiritual guru, but I can tell you with absolute certainty that we *all* need something to believe in. If you don't consciously choose your belief system, your belief system will unconsciously choose you. There's a powerful undertow of cultural messages, family of origin belief systems, and negative self-talk that can quickly drag you underwater. Spirituality is the surfboard that allows you to navigate the sometimes peaceful, sometimes perilous waves that life rolls your way.

⚷ You don't need to believe in a deity to be spiritual.

Baking, art, music, math, science, nature . . . anything that connects you to something greater than your own experience "counts" as spirituality. "A consensus among wisdom keepers from all the world's traditions suggest that human spirituality is a tightly woven integration of three facets: an insightful relationship with oneself and others, a strong personal value system, and the fulfillment of a meaningful purpose to one's life."[*]

⊶O Spirituality is *not* optional for wholeness and happiness.

Happiness is the feeling of home—home in your body, home in your mind, and home in your life. Until it feels like home *inside*, we'll continue to search for home *outside*—and psychological homesickness can't be healed by the people we love, the food we eat, or the things we buy. Your spirituality is the key to finding your way home to yourself. But spirituality neither needs to be religious nor boring. As *The Artist's Way* author and creative visionary Julia Cameron put it, "In filling the well, think magic. Think delight. Think fun. Do not think duty. Do not do what you should do—spiritual sit-ups like reading a dull but recommended critical text. Do what intrigues you, explore what interests you; think mystery, not mastery."

You are not here by accident, you are not a mistake, and your story is not over. As Deepak Chopra put it, "There are no extra pieces in the universe. Everyone is here because he or she has a place to fill, and every piece must fit itself into the big jigsaw puzzle."

Thank you for joining me on this journey. If you've made it this far, perhaps you're willing to take another step and see what happens next. After all . . .

There's more of you waiting to be discovered,
more to you than you realize exists,
and more for you than you ever dreamed possible.

---

[*] Brian Seaward, PhD, and Christine Lissard, RN, BSN, HN-BC, "A Spiritual Well-Being Model for the Healing Arts," *Journal of Holistic Nursing* 38, no. 1 (2020) 102–6, https://journals.sagepub.com/doi/10.1177/0898010120907528.

ACKNOWLEDGMENTS

A spark of an idea doesn't turn into a book without the help of countless people.

I am supremely grateful for the literary agent sorcery of Liza Dawson, Rachel Beck, Lynn Wu, and everyone at Liza Dawson Associates for believing in my work and guiding me through every step of the process. I cannot express enough thanks to my editor, Marian Lizzi, and the team at Penguin Random House for the skill and savvy it takes to bring books to life.

Thank you to my dear friend Vanessa Cornell and to the team of beautiful humans at NUSHU, as well as Amanda Baudier, Rashia Bell, Erika Bloom, Ally Bogard, Vienna Phaaron, and Rebecca Stump for their wisdom and feedback during the early stages of this project. Thank you to Nicole Whiting for being a fantastic otter friend and for the hours of strategy and encouragement. Thank you to Jenn Berry for your willingness to read pages and offer insights. Mega-thanks to my creative muse Sara Page for our years of friendship and for creating all the cartoons and icons in this book, and to Elise Reid for once again being a graphic designer superhero.

Thank you to Dr. Frank Anderson, Rick Kahler, Crystle Lampitt, and Madison Nicole for lending their words to this work, and to Dr. Richard Schwartz for creating the Internal Family Systems model—a model of therapy without which I would not be here today. Thank you to Julia Cameron for writing *The Artist's Way*—I'm forever changed because of Morning Pages. Thank you to all the teachers, mentors, and guides from whom I learned the art and science of psychotherapy, and to every therapy client who has ever walked into my office or popped up on my screen—thank you for trusting me with your story.

Respect to my husband, Mike, for challenging me to clarify ideas and sharpen my writing. Thank you for all the joy and laughter you bring to our life, and for being the best doggie dad to Oscar. I love you.

To the person reading this right now—whether we ever get to meet in this lifetime or not—thank you. I appreciate you more than words can say.

SUGGESTED READING

Anderson, Frank. *Transcending Trauma: Healing Complex PTSD with Internal Family Systems*. PESI Publishing, 2021.

Beaton, Connor. *Men's Work: A Practical Guide to Face Your Darkness, End Self-Sabotage, and Find Freedom*. Sounds True, 2023.

Beck, Martha. *The Way of Integrity: Finding the Path to Your True Self*. The Open Field, 2022.

Blades, Becky. *Start More Than You Can Finish: A Creative Permission Slip to Unleash Your Best Ideas*. Chronicle Prism, 2022.

Bolz-Weber, Nadia. *Shameless: A Case for Not Feeling Bad About Feeling Good (About Sex)*. Convergent Books, 2020.

Bradshaw, John. *Healing the Shame That Binds You*, expanded, updated edition. Health Communications, 2005.

Cameron, Julia. *The Artist's Way: A Spiritual Path to Higher Creativity*, 25th anniversary edition. TarcherPerigee, 2016.

Clear, James. *Atomic Habits: An Easy and Proven Way to Build Good Habits and Break Bad Ones*. Avery, 2018.

Dana, Deb. *The Polyvagal Theory in Therapy: Engaging the Rhythm of Regulation*. W. W. Norton, 2018.

Dann, Jordan. *Somatic Therapy for Healing Trauma: Effective Tools to Strengthen the Mind-Body Connection*. Rockridge Press, 2022.

Fern, Jessica. *Polysecure: Attachment, Trauma and Consensual Nonmonogamy*. Thornapple Press, 2020.

Goodman, Whitney. *Toxic Positivity: Keeping It Real in a World Obsessed with Being Happy*. Orion Spring, 2022.

Hari, Johann. *Lost Connections: Uncovering the Real Causes of Depression—and the Unexpected Solutions*. Bloomsbury, 2018.

Hendrix, Harville, and Helen LaKelly Hunt. *Getting the Love You Want: A Guide for Couples*, revised, updated edition. St. Martin's Griffin, 2019.

Lee, John. *Growing Yourself Back Up: Understanding Emotional Regression*. Three Rivers Press, 2001.

Levine, Peter A., and Ann Frederick. *Waking the Tiger: Healing Trauma*. North Atlantic Books, 1997.

McBride, Karyl. *Will I Ever Be Good Enough? Healing the Daughters of Narcissistic Mothers*. Atria Books, 2009.

McDaniel, Kelly. *Mother Hunger: How Adult Daughters Can Understand and Heal from Lost Nurturance, Protection, and Guidance*. Hay House, 2021.

McRaney, David. *How Minds Change: The Surprising Science of Belief, Opinion, and Persuasion*. Portfolio, 2022.

Miller, Alice. *The Drama of the Gifted Child: The Search for the True Self*, revised, updated edition, trans. Ruth Ward. Basic Books, 2007.

Mullan, Jennifer. *Decolonizing Therapy: Oppression, Historical Trauma, and Politicizing Your Practice*. W. W. Norton, 2023.

Nakazawa, Donna Jackson. *Childhood Disrupted: How Your Biography Becomes Your Biology, and How You Can Heal*. Atria Books, 2016.

O'Donohue, John. *Anam Cara: A Book of Celtic Wisdom*. Harper Perennial, 1998.

Pharaon, Vienna. *The Origin of You: How Breaking Family Patterns Can Liberate the Way We Live and Love*. G. P. Putnam's Sons, 2023.

Porges, Stephen. *The Pocket Guide to the Polyvagal Theory: The Transformative Power of Feeling Safe*. W. W. Norton, 2017.

Robinson, Bryan. *Chained to the Desk: A Guidebook for Workaholics, Their Partners and Children, and the Clinicians Who Treat Them*, third edition. New York University Press, 2014.

Schwartz, Richard. *No Bad Parts: Healing Trauma and Restoring Wholeness with the Internal Family Systems Model*. Sounds True, 2021.

Tawwab, Nedra. *Set Boundaries, Find Peace*. TarcherPerigee, 2021.

Taylor, Sonya Renee. *The Body Is Not an Apology: The Power of Radical Self-Love*, second edition. Berrett-Koehler, 2021.

Tribole, Evelyn, and Elyse Resch. *Intuitive Eating: A Revolutionary Anti-Diet Approach*, fourth edition. St. Martin's Essentials, 2020.

van der Kolk, Bessel. *The Body Keeps the Score: Brain, Mind, and Body in the Healing of Trauma*. Penguin, 2015.

Vora, Ellen. *The Anatomy of Anxiety: Understanding and Overcoming the Body's Fear Response*. Orion Spring, 2022.

White, Amanda E. *Not Drinking Tonight: A Guide to Creating a Sober Life You Love*. Hachette Go, 2022.

Wolynn, Mark. *It Didn't Start with You: How Inherited Family Trauma Shapes Who We Are and How to End the Cycle*. Penguin Life, 2017.

Britt Frank, MSW, LSCSW, SEP, is a licensed psychotherapist, speaker, and author of *The Science of Stuck*. She received her BA from Duke University and her MSW from the University of Kansas, where she later became an award-winning adjunct instructor. Frank speaks and writes widely about mental health, motivation, and how to change even the most long-standing patterns of thinking and doing.

◉ @brittfrank

Also by

Britt Frank